SOUTHE[RN] · TIMES ·

Contents

Front Cover: Motor fitted H class 0-4-4T No 31544 at Rowfant. No date but certainly late in life as per the second BR emblem and ever electrification warning flashes. The engine would survive in service until 1963; the station and line from Three Bridges to East Grinstead just four years longer. *Ken Wightman / Transport Treasury*

Left: Scotland or the West of England? The signals appear to be SR type, the spectacle plate of the engine in the distance is reminiscent of a Southern 'Mogul' but those asked are unwilling to commit to any particular location on 'The Withered Arm'. Readers thoughts are welcomed. *MP50420 / Transport Treasury*

Rear cover: Brand new Birmingham Railway carriage & Wagon Co. Diesel-electric No D6508 probably at Eastleigh around the time of delivery in May 1960. Seen here its its smart original livery, this engine migrated between Hither Green and Eastleigh during its working life subsequently being renumbered 33008 in April 1974 and having an active life of just short of 36 years before being withdrawn and condemned on 1 February 1996.

Copies of many of the images within SOUTHERN TIMES are available for purchase/download. Please quote the Issue, article, page number, and if shown the reference.

In addition the Transport Treasury Archive contains tens of thousands of other UK, Irish and some European railway photographs.

ISBN 978-1-913251-31-4

First Published in 2022 by Transport Treasury Publishing Ltd.,
16 Highworth Close, High Wycombe, HP13 7PJ

www.ttpublishing.co.uk *or for editorial issues and contributions email to* **SouthernTimes@email.com**

Printed in Tarxien, Malta by Gutenberg Press Ltd.

INTRODUCTION

Welcome to Issue 2 of Southern Times. We will admit to having been somewhat staggered by the positive reaction we have had between the release of Issue 1 and the need to complete Issue 2 ready for release just three months later.

As a matter of course most of the content of Issue 2 was set before the first issue was received from print and likewise we aim to be well on the way to having No 3 ready by the time you read this. Sometimes it might almost feel as if we are painting the Forth Bridge as when reaching the end we have to start all over again – but do excuse the analogy as we don't think by any stretch of the imagination we could pretend there is a linking connection with Scotland. Or is there? In 'Western Times' the companion journal to 'ST', our colleague Andrew Malthouse recently penned a piece on the Western Region 16xx class Pannier tanks that ended working far from home at The Mound.

This got us thinking, did any Southern engines ever venture that far north? Whereupon, and genuinely by chance whilst delving in the Transport Treasury archive, we came across a negative packet labelled 'E1/R class 0-6-2T No 32096? Scotland? June 1954.' The view was in the Transport Treasury 'Milepost' collection. So, the obvious questions, is the location correct, and if so what was the E1/R doing there? (Answers on a postcard please....no seriously, if anyone can enlighten us, do please let us know.) The view is shown opposite.

Away from hypothesis, we genuinely hope you similarly enjoy Issue 2. Compiling and producing ST has given us the opportunity to indulge more into what we hope readers want using the feedback from issue 1 – so do please let us know if it is about right.

We welcome your comments, and if you would like, your contributions, in article or image form.

We hope you enjoy this issue and look forward to working on Issue 3.

Robin Fell and the Transport Treasury Publishing Team

Look out for Southern Times Issue 3 in September 2022.

Content to include:

The demise of the 'Lord Nelson' class
Riding the 'Rivers'
More colour from S C Townroe
The LSWR A12 0-4-2 class
Deptford Wharf Part 2
Southern electric pictorial
Guildford to Horsham
Abnormal load
Southern power signal box exteriors
Southern Allocations: Dover, Faversham, Gillingham, Maidstone East, Maidstone West, Ramsgate.

and of course lots more!

34002

Smoke deflectors (and deflection) on the 'Light Pacifics'

As is widely known, there were 110 Light Pacifics built by the Southern Railway and Southern Region, 110 engines which to all intents were identical and split into two 'classes', ('West Country' and 'Battle of Britain') but which subsequently also varied over time according to original or rebuilt state, plus of course minor changes to equipment fitted.

In this brief resume we are concerned with only one aspect of the type; the smoke deflector variations, plus the experiments that persisted intermittently almost from the debut of the first of the class through until the early 1960s.

In order to place these changes in perspective we must first look back at their larger and older cousins, the 'Merchant Navy' class, where it was quickly found that drifting steam could easily create difficulties with forward vision. Most Southern lines on which steam was used ran east-west so meaning the prevailing winds would not tend to blow exhaust steam sideways. The exception to this was between Basingstoke and Southampton where the route runs south to reach the coast before resuming its east-west course.

Various experiments with the front end design of the 'Merchant Navy' class had previously been attempted before a compromise in the shape of a hood and side smoke deflectors was arrived at; not ideal but it served the purpose, that is until the whole class were subsequently rebuilt.

The Light Pacifics copied this compromise design from the outset with the slight advantage that their smaller boiler meant they were slimmer at the waist, although from a distance both designs were in many respects so similar it was sometimes only when the shape of the nameplate, the engine number, or when viewed head-on could positive identification be made. In the latter case, the original 'Merchant Navy' type were noticeably more bulbous.

In practice it was not long before complaints of drifting smoke and steam concerning the Light Pacifics reached the ears of management. The problem with modern large engines being their softer exhaust tended not to throw the exhaust high enough into the air to keep it clear of the cab, this was especially so when working with an early cut-off.

Such were the complaints as to poor visibility that as early as November 1946 Nos 21C137, 21C139, 21C141 and 21C142 were seen working with lengths of coloured tape attached to the smoke deflectors whilst on board cameras recorded the results. When the films were viewed the results indicated there was insufficient lift being created by the original short deflectors and a longer variant was proposed. Accordingly, just a few weeks later, in January 1947, No 21C108 was tested with long deflectors, according to Bradley for just one day between Redhill and Tonbridge but even so with positive results.

Two other engines, Nos 21C122 and 21C140, were similarly modified in February 1947 and when once again the improvement was confirmed the long deflectors became standard for the class – presumably as they passed through works. Do not confuse what was then referred to as long with the extra-long deflectors subsequently fitted to Nos 34004, 34005 and 34006. These were provided when the engines were being made ready for use, or stand by, for the 1948 interchange trials. It is also interesting to note that when a change – or reversion did take place, this does not appear to be mentioned on the engine record cards whereas another change to the earlier series, for example the wedge fronted cab, is however recorded.

Opposite: Extreme circumstances, No 34002 *Salisbury* engulfed in steam possibly in consequence of a slip. Clearly any forward vision is lost even temporarily - thank goodness then for the AWS box at the front. *The Transport Treasury*

'Tweaking' of the design to perhaps afford an even greater improvement took place on No 21C162 in May 1947 and in this and the following month the engine ran with the leading ends of the deflectors curved inwards. No improvement was noted and it reverted to standard pattern. Unfortunately no images of these early changes have been discovered, especially so in the case of the last mentioned. No 21C162, in the way it is described by Bradley, although it sounds not dissimilar to the later change made to No 34035 in December 1959.

Subsequently the extra long smoke deflectors were removed from all but one member of the class, No 34006, which retained these through to withdrawal. Nos 34004 and 34005 loosing these at the time of rebuilding.

What results might have been obtained on Nos 34004-6 is not detailed but clearly insufficient benefit to warrant their general adoption on the rest of the engines. Possibly it was to maximise advantage gained purely for the interchange trials mentioned. As to why the long deflectors were not copied is a slight puzzle as the same drifting smoke and steam issues still prevailed and it has been

The three variations:

Above: Original short deflectors as fitted to No 21C114 *Budleigh Salterton* posed for its official portrait. The initial design of cab front and two side windows will be noted; the white buffers also, although the latter were not always a regular sight in official views - but do also see p80.

Opposite top: No 34093 *Saunton* at Brighton fresh from overhaul, probably January 1956; 'medium' length deflectors. (An excellent 'step by step' article on the rebuilding of this engine, appears in the Winter 2021/22 issue of *Bulleid Express* (the journal of the Bulleid Society and the Bluebell Railway Battle of Britain group.)

Opposite bottom: No 34005 *Barnstaple,* one of the engines to be fitted with the extra long deflector plates. Sister No 34006 retained this style through to the end. *The Transport Treasury*

34093

34005
BARNSTAPLE
34005

No 34092 *City of Wells* displaying the more usual effect of drifting smoke and steam, taken at 9.52am on 16 October 1960 at Bromley. In its later preserved form this engine has been fitted with a Giesl ejector of the same type as was installed by BR on No 34064. *Dave B. Clark / The Transport Treasury*

suggested that inadequate forward vision was a contributory factor in the terrible accident at Lewisham of December 1957 although it must also be said that fog was another issue on that occasion.

Possibly it was the repercussions of Lewisham that led to the final attempts at improving smoke lifting and visibility on the original design. Two engines were involved, Nos 34035 and 34049, both also somewhat camera shy during this period. Bradley aptly describes the change to both as, 'the removal of the smoke deflector plates and the joining of the side casing to the front cowling, thereby giving the front end a more rounded appearance.'

Whilst No 34049 reverted to conventional type (that is if an original Bulleid Pacific could ever be described as conventional) in February 1960, No 34035 was the subject of a further experiment with the deflectors restored but then turned in at the front end – as per the accompanying image. With the front curved as mentioned it can certainly have done nothing to enhance the crew's view forward. The changes to No 34035 at this time sound similar to those tried on 21C162 back in 1947; perhaps someone thought they could do better 12 years later.

No 34035 was retained as a guinea pig a while longer than its sister. Subsequently it is believed it too was restored to standard form but this cannot be completely confirmed as it was destined to be an early casualty for withdrawal in June 1963. What we do know is that No 34035 was photographed working on the South Eastern section in its modified form certainly in 1960 although nowhere does it appear to have been allocated to a South Eastern depot. Instead it remained an

Beauty can hardly have been in the minds of the Eastleigh drawing office when this adjustment was made to Nos 34035 and 34049 in December 1959. Regretfully no views have been found of either engine at work in this form. Might the slots in the side even have performed a dual function; as hand holds to assist when climbing on to the front foot plating and to catch the air and direct it upwards? *Southampton Model Railway Society*

Exmouth Junction machine until withdrawn and consequently was a long way from home. We can only speculate as to why the distance between Eastleigh and its known workings; not wanted by Exmouth Junction, being observed by a London based inspector or even 'out of sight, out of mind'. It is especially interesting to note that no photos have emerged of a modified No 34035 working a service that in any way could have originated or been destined towards Exmouth Junction. Possibly it was simple experimentation which in the end was not considered worthwhile pursuing in consequence of the limited life that remained for steam. Some records though must have been kept but sadly these appear not to have survived.

One other experiment was carried out on the original engines and as late as 1962, which was the fitting of a Giesl ejector to No 34064. Folklore has it that this fitment had the effect of lifting the exhaust high into the air and at the same time made this particular Light Pacific the equivalent of a Merchant Navy. Bradley however contradicts this with the words, '(No 34064 was so fitted)....apparently to offset the loss of efficiency caused by the addition of a spark-arrestor rather than to evaluate the improvement in fuel consumption. No official trials were run, but correspondence found at Eastleigh Works (and presumably also lost forever - Ed), suggests that the steaming proved erratic and that most crews found the firing more difficult and the slipping more noticeable. To the lineside observer the acceleration was poor and the unevenness of the Bulleid valve gear more pronounced.' John Click, Assistant Works Manager at Eastleigh at the time, had a different take on the converted No 34064: 'In service the engine was a cracker, it threw no sparks, and, as we had

34035
30861

34035

Opposite top: A chance image captured from Campbell Road bridge at Eastleigh. The photographer has not recorded the date but from the clean condition of No 30861, which was 'inside' in December 1961, and the time of year confirmed by the leafless trees outside the office block, it is reasonable to assume this was indeed around the period stated. Notice that No 34035 is devoid of its nameplate but clearly displays the second attempt at improving air flow. Southern green dominates almost as far as the eye can see. *The Transport Treasury*

Opposite bottom: Workaday grime for No 34035 working the 'Man of Kent' at Ramsgate on 10 May 1960, the driver behaving as anticipated with his head outside the window. With no visible exhaust we cannot judge if the modification was a success in traffic but it is still interesting to note that no other engines were similarly modified. Date and location, apart from SE section, are not given. *Dave B. Clark / The Transport Treasury*

Above: No 34035 outside Eastleigh works. Stored / withdrawn, we do not know although judging by the rust, clearly not having moved for a time.

bargained, lifted its smoke in a way that none of the other 139 engines did, altered or not.'

Sadly, it was too late in the day for this to have any effect on the other Bulleid engines, especially as BRB at Marylebone had been none too impressed with the results obtained at Rugby with the solitary Giesl fitted BR Standard 9F, No 92250.

As to why certain engines were selected for trials and not others is simply explained; usually they happened to be conveniently available at the time. Also to be taken into account was that occasionally one member of a class might gain a reputation, whether deserved or not, for being poor at steaming or such like; in which case a shed master was only willing to give up his lame duck to the experimental section.

In summary it is interesting to note that so far as the Southern was concerned, smoke lifting had been considered a problem many years earlier, the Lord Nelson, Schools, King Arthur, H15, S15, N, U, N1 and U1 Moguls all retro fitted with smoke deflectors back in SR days. Further afield and also in BR days experimentation with methods of smoke lifting was going on simultaneously on the Eastern Region, various members of the A3 class fitted with either German type half deflectors or small wings either side of the chimney.

34064
72 A
SPL

Ryde Pier Head Tram

The above view is the second, and final rail related view loaned to us for use from a small collection of glass plates in the possession of Chris Richardson. We were able to identify the location at once, but the actual vehicle was a bit of puzzler.

A brief note to one of the acknowledged IOW experts, Roger Silsbury elucidated the following detailed reply;

'The photo you attached is not a Starbuck tram, but was originally the Lancaster C&W Co 45ft long, 6-wheel motor car built in 1892, which proved to wear hard on the track, so in 1907 was cut into two halves, making a motor car and a trailer, which ran on the west track on the pier. They lasted until the advent of the petrol cars in 1927, when they were withdrawn and scrapped.'

Also of interest is the signal on the right with its stop and distant arms. This signal does not appear on the diagrams produced by the Signalling Record Society or in the John Wagstaff collection and consequently it is likely we may then assess the time frame as being nearer the first of Roger's dates.

The section from Ryde Esplanade - platforms on the right - and Pier Head stallions was short, indeed the home signals for Pier Head may be seen in the distance.

Note too both the stop and distant arms are painted red; yellow for distant signals was not introduced until c1927 onwards.

Opposite: The ultimate attempt at clearing smoke and steam. No 34064 *Fighter Command* paused in Wallers Ash Loop on its first trial from Eastleigh after the fitting of a Giesl ejector. Top left – loco crew and then John Click, Assistant Works Manager, Eastleigh. Lower left – loco crew, fitter, Harry Frith, Eastleigh Erecting Shop Foreman. The oblong fitment of the elector itself is visible through the top cowling. It is believed this was a light engine run so it must have been a bit crowded on the footplate. No 34064 ran in this form for two years from 1962 until withdrawn in 1964. *John Click*

Interlude around Midhurst

Looking through the photo archive at Transport Treasury it can sometimes be easy to settle upon a theme for a photo article – equally sometimes not quite so easy when a required but elusive view is just not to be found.

One of the successful forays of recent times concerned the R. E. Vincent collection which was found to contain a number of images of Midhurst; a station which lost its passenger service 67 years ago and yet was once served by two different companies with lines in three directions.

Roy visited the station on three occasions and in consecutive years, 1950, 1951 and 1952, possibly coinciding with military service at nearby Longmoor. We have also added three views from other photographers to present a more complete portrayal.

Top: The eastern extend of Midhurst branch services, Pulborough, where No 30108 replenishes its tanks after arrival with the single coach 12.40pm through service from Petersfield on the last day of 1954. Scenes such as this would last for only a few more weeks as passenger trains ceased on the branch from 5 February 1955. ***Graham Smith courtesy Richard Sissons***

Bottom: Our first view on the branch proper and another through service from Petersfield to Pulborough behind M7 No 30481, recorded by Farnham based photographer E. C. Griffiths leaving Selham on 5 June 1951. The rural nature of all the lines serving Midhurst is emphasised here with limited passenger traffic and no major industry or major conurbation to provide for regular and sustained traffic.

Opposite: From the east M7 No 30056 is about to enter the tunnel immediately preceding the station with a 2-coach pull-push working from Pulborough terminating at Midhurst. No confirmed date, but the listing either side shows May and July 1951; likely to be closer to July as the driver has the end window open to catch the breeze. ***Ref: 56/ C/2/2***

MIDHURST
From Petersfield
L.&S.W. STA.
5c
6c
JUNCTION
21c
JUNC.
5c
L.B.&S.C. STA.
To Petworth
From Chichester
726

Opposite top: From the hillside on the station side of the tunnel we gain a panoramic view of the site. Approaching and bound for Billingshurst, Fittleworth and Pulborough is C2X No 32550 on a freight for Pulborough, 25 May 1951. The high vantage point is an opportunity to describe the railway geography and history of the area, starting with the line from Pulborough which reached Midhurst from the east, terminating at the station seen behind the brake van. Follow the course of the railway into the distance and a solitary coach may be seen parked. Beyond this on the right was the former LSWR terminus at Midhurst where services would once arrive from Petersfield. Until after the grouping in 1923 there was no through passenger service between the two companies; passengers wishing to continue their journey east (or west) having to alight from one train and make their own way to the opposing station. A siding for the exchange of goods was however provided. Between the two stations and just identified by the curving tree line, was another LBSCR route south through Cocking, Singleton and Lavant to Chichester. Despite Singleton affording easy access to Goodwood racecourse, patronage was poor and the route closed to passengers in the 1930s. It remained open as a through route for freight until a culvert collapsed early into BR days severing the line. It was not reinstated. Post-grouping the LSWR station was closed, and a proper connection provided between the LSWR and LBSCR lines, all passenger traffic concentrated at the former LBSCR site. Passenger services were a mixture of through Pulborough to Petersfield services and also short workings from either end terminating at Midhurst. *Ref: 56/C/2/1*

Opposite bottom: Eastwards departure, locomotive leading pull-push set No 731, 30 June 1950. Despite, it must be said, being very much a rural backwater, some modern Southern infrastructure is present including the upper quadrant starting signal (the home signal is definitely of an older vintage) and concrete lamp post. Standard Southern Railway warning notices have also appeared. *Ref: REV1 (1867)*

Above: Single coach train departing. Passenger traffic suffered badly at Midhurst in consequence of developing road competition, those who desired to travel east or west were catered for – albeit at infrequent intervals – but south there was no passenger service and north meant going east or west first. Small wonder then that the end came some years before the good Doctor wielded his scalpel – in 1955. *Ref: REV1 (2331)*

Above: On the same day as when we saw No 30108 at Pulborough earlier, we witness a crossing movement at Midhurst. No 30108 on the right will take its train east, whilst on the left M7 No 30027 waits to depart, propelling its pull-push working west to Petersfield. The lack of any obvious fare paying passengers is the tell-tale sign (the man seen being in railway uniform). Notice the typical LBSCR feature of a subway linking the two platforms. *Graham Smith courtesy Richard Sissons*

Opposite top: Looking through the station, which displays all the appearance of a main thoroughfare. The M7, No 30048, and pull-push set is waiting in the Petersfield bay, the Guard intent on loading – or is it unloading? One potential passenger enjoys the sun, even if he travels, the revenue accrued will do little to contribute to running costs. No exact date, but almost certainly June/July 1952. *Ref: 67/C/6/2*

Above: In the process of and leaving Midhurst; propelling back towards Petersfield. One passenger at least enjoying the fresh air, and when propelling there was no chance of smuts in the eye either. Midhurst signal box is in the background and which replaced the original LSWR and LBSCR structures when the two lines were conjoined. The former LBSCR structure which stood at the east end of the same platform was retained and found a new use as an office for the incumbent station master. *Ref: 67/C/6/3*

Southern Times welcomes contributions, articles, images, comments etc.

Please contact the Transport Treasury editorial address.

Top: Our final view of Midhurst depicts a pull-push service arriving into the former LBSCR platform from Petersfield – obviously a through working to Pulborough. LBSCR signals abound but these were replaced by a standard lattice gantry later. ***Ref: REV1 (1861)***

Bottom: The slightly unusual perspective from the cab of a C2X 0-6-0 (no engine number given) approaching the 443 yard West Dean tunnel just south of Singleton at a time when the line up from Chichester was in operation. ***H. M. Madgwick***

Less glamorous times on the Chichester line. Another C2X, this time BR No 32550, standing by, waiting to assist in the recovery of sister engine No 32522 which had fallen into a collapsed culvert in late 1951. *S. C. Townroe*

Westward destination at Petersfield where there was a separate platform for Midhurst branch train on the north side of the level crossing deliberately placed to avoid conflict with the main line. Again set No 731 but also devoid of a route disc – but then everyone knew this was the branch service. Visit the same scene today and apart from the pair of electrified main lines on the left all else has vanished. Wonderful pole route! *Ref: 61/C/6/2*

Southern Allocations - Eastern Section 1934
Part 1: Ashford, Battersea, and Bricklayers Arms

From records compiled by the late Alan Elliott

	Ashford						
735	A1X	0-6-0T		1402	N	2-6-0	
955	Z	0-8-0T		1403	N	2-6-0	
1002	F1	4-4-0		1404	N	2-6-0	
1010	R1	0-6-0T		1426	N	2-6-0	
1011	F1	4-4-0		1477	D	4-4-0	
1047	R1	0-6-0T		1488	D	4-4-0	
1065	O1	0-6-0		1490	D	4-4-0	
1080	O1	0-6-0		1521	H	0-4-4T	
1105	F1	4-4-0		1522	H	0-4-4T	
1124	R	0-6-0T		1549	D	4-4-0	
1126	R	0-6-0T		1558	P	0-6-0T	
1137	F1	4-4-0		1583	C	0-6-0	
1140	F1	4-4-0		1589	C	0-6-0	
1151	F1	4-4-0		1664	R	0-4-4T	Motor train fitted
1191	C	0-6-0		1671	R	0-4-4T	Motor train fitted
1201	F1	4-4-0		1703	R1	0-6-0T	
1218	C	0-6-0		1726	D	4-4-0	
1245	C	0-6-0		1740	D	4-4-0	
1272	C	0-6-0		1772	L	4-4-0	
1306	H	0-4-4T		1773	L	4-4-0	
1336	R	0-6-0T		1774	L	4-4-0	
1338	R	0-6-0T		1775	L	4-4-0	
1385	O1	0-6-0		1776	L	4-4-0	
1400	N	2-6-0		1800	U	2-6-0	
1401	N	2-6-0		1803	U	2-6-0	

T class 0-6-0T No 1604, allocated to Battersea in 1933. Previously known as Battersea and before that Longhedge, the name was changed to Stewarts Lane consequent upon the rebuilding of the shed in 1933.

	Battersea									
281	T9	4-4-0		1165	E1	4-4-0		1684	C	0-6-0
282	T9	4-4-0		1177	H	0-4-4T		1685	S	0-6-0ST
300	T9	4-4-0		1179	E1	4-4-0		1705	R1	0-4-4T
301	T9	4-4-0		1195	F1	4-4-0		1706	R1	0-4-4T
303	T9	4-4-0		1240	F1	4-4-0		1712	C	0-6-0
304	T9	4-4-0		1250	F1	4-4-0		1714	C	0-6-0
307	T9	4-4-0		1266	H	0-4-4T		1716	C	0-6-0
310	T9	4-4-0		1319	H	0-4-4T		1718	C	0-6-0
311	T9	4-4-0		1321	H	0-4-4T		1720	C	0-6-0
312	T9	4-4-0		1328	H	0-4-4T		1722	C	0-6-0
314	T9	4-4-0		1495	C	0-6-0		1724	C	0-6-0
704	T9	4-4-0		1497	E1	4-4-0		1767	L	4-4-0
726	T9	4-4-0		1498	C	0-6-0		1768	L	4-4-0
763	N15	4-6-0		1499	C	0-6-0		1769	L	4-4-0
764	N15	4-6-0		1503	H	0-4-4T		1770	L	4-4-0
765	N15	4-6-0		1504	E1	4-4-0		1771	L	4-4-0
766	N15	4-6-0		1506	E1	4-4-0		1862	N	2-6-0
767	N15	4-6-0		1507	E1	4-4-0		1863	N	2-6-0
770	N15	4-6-0		1508	C	0-6-0		1864	N	2-6-0
771	N15	4-6-0		1511	E1	4-4-0		1866	N	2-6-0
772	N15	4-6-0		1513	C	0-6-0		1867	N	2-6-0
793	N15	4-6-0		1517	H	0-4-4T		1868	N	2-6-0
794	N15	4-6-0		1533	H	0-4-4T		1869	N	2-6-0
795	N15	4-6-0		1548	H	0-4-4T		1870	N	2-6-0
796	N15	4-6-0		1573	C	0-6-0		1875	N	2-6-0
850	LN	4-6-0		1575	C	0-6-0		1890	U1	2-6-0
851	LN	4-6-0		1576	C	0-6-0		1901	U1	2-6-0
852	LN	4-6-0		1578	C	0-6-0		1902	U1	2-6-0
853	LN	4-6-0		1579	C	0-6-0		1903	U1	2-6-0
854	LN	4-6-0		1580	C	0-6-0		1904	U1	2-6-0
855	LN	4-6-0		1581	C	0-6-0		1905	U1	2-6-0
856	LN	4-6-0		1582	C	0-6-0		1906	U1	2-6-0
858	LN	4-6-0		1588	C	0-6-0		1907	U1	2-6-0
859	LN	4-6-0		1590	C	0-6-0		1908	U1	2-6-0
963	LN	4-6-0		1600	T	0-6-0T		1909	U1	2-6-0
864	LN	4-6-0		1601	T	0-6-0T		1910	U1	2-6-0
1005	H	0-4-4T		1602	T	0-6-0T		1911	W	2-6-4T
1019	E1	4-4-0		1603	T	0-6-0T		1912	W	2-6-4T
1062	E1	4-4-0		1604	T	0-6-0T		1913	W	2-6-4T
1067	E1	4-4-0		1606	T	0-6-0T		1914	W	2-6-4T
1089	F1	4-4-0		1607	T	0-6-0T		1915	W	2-6-4T
1149	E1	4-4-0		1608	T	0-6-0T		2021	I3	4-4-2T
1160	E1	4-4-0		1609	T	0-6-0T		2022	I3	4-4-2T
1163	E1	4-4-0		1661	R	0-4-4T		2023	I3	4-4-2T
1164	H	0-4-4T		1683	C	0-6-0		2025	I3	4-4-2T

One of three Z class tank engines allocated to Bricklayers Arms depot in 1933. For many years the depot had freight as its principal responsibility.

Another Battersea resident, W No 1911. The similarity with the SECR 'K' class depicted elsewhere in this issue will be noted although the W was fitted with smaller driving wheels and did not have the derived drive for the middle cylinder taken from the outside.

	Battersea cont.									
2049	B4	4-4-0		2404	E5	0-6-2T		2490	E4	0-6-2T
2051	B4	4-4-0		2407	E6X	0-6-2T		2492	E4	0-6-2T
2064	B4	4-4-0		2408	E6	0-6-2T		2496	E4	0-6-2T
2081	I3	4-4-2T		2409	E6	0-6-2T		2497	E4	0-6-2T
2090	I3	4-4-2T		2410	E6	0-6-2T		2532	C2X	0-6-0
2101	E2	0-6-0T		2411	E6X	0-6-2T		2535	C2X	0-6-0
2102	E2	0-6-0T		2412	E6	0-6-2T		2536	C2X	0-6-0
2105	E2	0-6-0T		2413	E6X	0-6-2T		2541	C2X	0-6-0
2198	E2	0-6-0T		2440	C2X	0-6-0		2542	C2X	0-6-0
2337	K	2-6-0		2444	C2X	0-6-0		2549	C2X	0-6-0
2338	K	2-6-0		2447	C2X	0-6-0		2556	E4	0-6-2T
2340	K	2-6-0		2451	C2X	0-6-0		2564	E4	0-6-2T
2341	K	2-6-0		2484	E4	0-6-2T				

Eleven of the Lord Nelson class were at Battersea in 1933 for working boat trains between London and the Kent Coast at the time in question so as per the comments about the demise of the class in the accompanying article, no doubt Battersea men were indeed familiar with the firing technique required. No 859 *Lord Hood* seen here before the addition of smoke deflectors.

One of 18 members of the former SECR E class allocated to Bricklayers Arms in 1933, No 1275 is depicted at the depot two years later in 1935. ***ERW 932***

In SECR days and before the addition of '1000' to the number, Bricklayers Arms based B1 (?) is seen with a mixed SECR rake behind the tender.

	Bricklayers Arms									
950	Z	0-8-0T		1277	C	0-6-0		1544	H	0-4-4T
951	Z	0-8-0T		1280	C	0-6-0		1546	H	0-4-4T
956	Z	0-8-0T		1287	C	0-6-0		1547	E	4-4-0
1018	C	0-6-0		1291	C	0-6-0		1550	H	0-4-4T
1033	C	0-6-0		1294	C	0-6-0		1551	H	0-4-4T
1036	E	4-4-0		1315	E	4-4-0		1552	H	0-4-4T
1038	C	0-6-0		1317	C	0-6-0		1587	E	4-4-0
1039	O1	0-6-0		1326	H	0-4-4T		1592	C	0-6-0
1046	O1	0-6-0		1327	H	0-4-4T		1593	C	0-6-0
1051	O1	0-6-0		1370	O1	0-6-0		1595	J	0-6-4T
1061	C	0-6-0		1374	O1	0-6-0		1596	J	0-6-4T
1068	C	0-6-0		1377	O1	0-6-0		1597	J	0-6-4T
1071	C	0-6-0		1380	O1	0-6-0		1598	J	0-6-4T
1093	O1	0-6-0		1381	O1	0-6-0		1599	J	0-6-4T
1102	C	0-6-0		1383	O1	0-6-0		1687	C	0-6-0
1112	C	0-6-0		1384	O1	0-6-0		1689	C	0-6-0
1113	C	0-6-0		1386	O1	0-6-0		1690	C	0-6-0
1132	B1	4-4-0		1388	O1	0-6-0		1691	C	0-6-0
1157	E	4-4-0		1389	O1	0-6-0		1694	C	0-6-0
1159	E	4-4-0		1391	O1	0-6-0		1695	C	0-6-0
1162	H	0-4-4T		1395	O1	0-6-0		1711	C	0-6-0
1166	E	4-4-0		1397	O1	0-6-0		1715	C	0-6-0
1175	E	4-4-0		1398	O1	0-6-0		1717	C	0-6-0
1176	E	4-4-0		1428	O1	0-6-0		1719	C	0-6-0
1223	C	0-6-0		1438	O1	0-6-0		1721	C	0-6-0
1224	O1	0-6-0		1440	B1	4-4-0		1753	L1	4-4-0
1251	O1	0-6-0		1453	B1	4-4-0		1754	L1	4-4-0
1258	O1	0-6-0		1454	B1	4-4-0		1755	L1	4-4-0
1268	C	0-6-0		1455	B1	4-4-0		1756	L1	4-4-0
1270	C	0-6-0		1456	B1	4-4-0		1757	L1	4-4-0
1273	E	4-4-0		1457	B1	4-4-0		1758	L1	4-4-0
1275	E	4-4-0		1459	B1	4-4-0		1759	L1	4-4-0
1514	E	4-4-0		1460	C	0-6-0		1782	L1	4-4-0
1515	E	4-4-0		1481	C	0-6-0		1783	L1	4-4-0
1516	E	4-4-0		1491	E	4-4-0		1784	L1	4-4-0
1540	H	0-4-4T		1500	H	0-4-4T		1785	L1	4-4-0
1541	H	0-4-4T		1514	E	4-4-0		1786	L1	4-4-0
1542	H	0-4-4T		1515	E	4-4-0		1787	L1	4-4-0
1544	H	0-4-4T		1516	E	4-4-0		1788	L1	4-4-0
1546	H	0-4-4T		1540	H	0-4-4T		1789	L1	4-4-0
1547	E	4-4-0		1541	H	0-4-4T		1811	N	2-6-0
1550	H	0-4-4T		1542	H	0-4-4T		1813	N	2-6-0

	Bricklayers Arms cont.									
1814	N	2-6-0		1821	N	2-6-0		2162	E1	0-6-0T
1815	N	2-6-0		1822	N1	2-6-0		2165	E3	0-6-2T
1816	N	2-6-0		1823	N	2-6-0		2168	E3	0-6-2T
1817	N	2-6-0		1865	N	2-6-0		2453	E3	0-6-2T
1818	N	2-6-0		2092	B4	2-6-0		2461	E3	0-6-2T
1819	N	2-6-0		2113	E1	0-6-0T		2462	E3	0-6-2T
1820	N	2-6-0								

Above: The unique 'S' class 0-6-0ST No 685 (later 1685), rebuilt in this form from a 'C' class tender engine. It was allocated to Battersea.

Opposite top: No 766 *Sir Geraint*, another Battersea resident. Note the vacuum pump below the crosshead.

Opposite bottom: Finally 'C' class 0-6-0 No 1071, one of a number of 'C' and 'O1' class 0-6-0 tender engines used principally on goods workings from Bricklayers Arms.

To be continued in Issue 3 featuring the 1933 allocations at Dover, Faversham, Gillingham, Maidstone East, Maidstone West, and Ramsgate.

766
SOUTHERN

1071
SOUTHERN

The Deptford Wharf Branch, Part 1
Alan Postlethwaite

Opening in 1704, Deptford Wharf was originally a private boat yard owned by the Evelyn family. Between 1783 and 1812, twenty-three Royal Navy warships and two East Indiamen were launched (*Ref. Wikipedia*). Convicts were also exported to Australia. The yard was taken over by the LBSCR, opening in 1849 with rail connections to Old Kent Road and to both sides of New Cross Gate. Imports included timber from Scandinavia, coal from NE England and general goods. Latterly, coal became dominant with many trains daily to the gas works and power stations on Waddon Marsh, near West Croydon. The wharf was also used for empty stock and parcels reversals to and from the Down side of New Cross Gate. The branch closed in 1964 and the wharf has since been redeveloped with housing and offices.

This first part looks at both ends of the branch. In the next issue of *Southern Times,* Part 2 will unravel the Cold Blow Tangle in the middle ground.

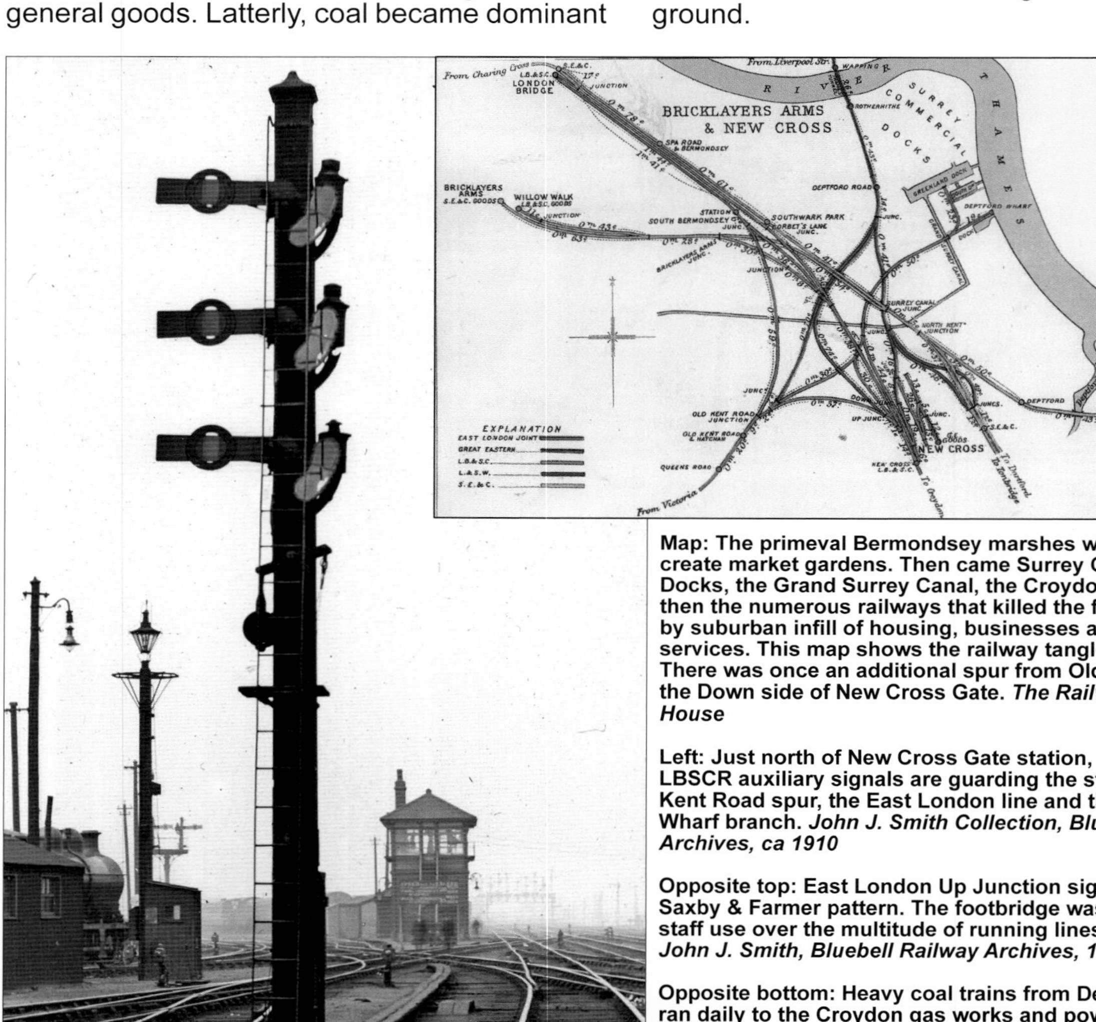

Map: The primeval Bermondsey marshes were drained to create market gardens. Then came Surrey Commercial Docks, the Grand Surrey Canal, the Croydon Canal and then the numerous railways that killed the farms, followed by suburban infill of housing, businesses and public services. This map shows the railway tangle in 1908. There was once an additional spur from Old Kent Road to the Down side of New Cross Gate. *The Railway Clearing House*

Left: Just north of New Cross Gate station, these stately LBSCR auxiliary signals are guarding the starts of the Old Kent Road spur, the East London line and the Deptford Wharf branch. *John J. Smith Collection, Bluebell Railway Archives, ca 1910*

Opposite top: East London Up Junction signal box was of Saxby & Farmer pattern. The footbridge was provided for staff use over the multitude of running lines and sidings. *John J. Smith, Bluebell Railway Archives, 1961*

Opposite bottom: Heavy coal trains from Deptford Wharf ran daily to the Croydon gas works and power stations. Passing through Brockley, this one has picked up a banker (E2 class 0-6-0T No 32104) at New Cross Gate for the 1 in 100 ascent of Forest Hill bank. The railway's predecessor, the Croydon Canal, needed 23 locks for this ascent. The 4-SUB unit is a Bulleid type and the goods brake is LBSCR. *John J. Smith, Bluebell Railway Archives, 1957*

90

New Cross Gate grew from a humble country station into a major LBSCR railway centre. Looking south, the track on the right (second one up) is the start of the Deptford Wharf Up line. On the left, the track to the right of the ground signal is the Deptford Wharf Down line. Seen here is an East London arrival from Liverpool Street headed by 0-4-4 condensing tank No LT 44. Beyond the train is the general goods yard and beyond that the former Great Eastern coal yard. On the far right are carriage sidings and the former MPD that closed in 1947. *John J. Smith, Bluebell Railway Archives, 1961*

The sunken coal yard at New Cross Gate. The 1871 OS map shows this dip full of water as the southern limit of the Croydon Canal. The incline on the left is the start of the lower line to Deptford Wharf. There were once coking ovens to the left of the camera and further ovens beyond the bridge carrying the Up spur to the East London line and Old Kent Road. *Alan Postlethwaite, Bluebell Railway Archives, 1958*

On what was washing day, a somewhat murky and grimy scene near Deptford Park featuring E3 0-6-2T No 32459 in charge of a coal train on the ascent out of Deptford Wharf. *John J. Smith, Bluebell Railway Archives, 1954*

On the final approach to Deptford Wharf is a rail tour from London Bridge on 29 March 1958 to a destination abbreviated by the late John Smith as 'BH' (*probably 'Blackheath - Ed. See the very useful 'Six Bells Junction' Railtour site for full details).* Propelled by H class 0-4-4T No 31518, at the head is pull-push set No 657, formerly of LSWR stock. *John J. Smith, Bluebell Railway, Archives, 1958.*

Deptford Wharf's Dudman's Dock looking south with travelling jib cranes and a grassy siding. *John J. Smith, Bluebell Railway Archives, 1957*

Coal, coal and yet more coal but not a soul in sight. Similarly wagons everywhere, including a buffer truck on the right. In LBSCR days, the three-way point on the right had been a four-way turnout. It is likely that horses were originally employed here to help with the shunting. *Lens of Sutton, Dennis Callum Collection, 1958*

The South rail entrance to Deptford Wharf featuring a Saxby & Farmer signal box, tall silos on the left, an overhead conveyor, cranes, plenty of mineral wagons and a huddle of visiting enthusiasts. Are any of them even reading this? *A.E. Bennett, The Transport Treasury, 1959*

In 1900, a tramway opened along Grove Street using a petrol locomotive. It ran from Deptford Wharf to the City of London's Foreign Cattle Market. When the latter became the Army's Reserve Supply Depot during the First World War, the tramway was rebuilt to take steam locomotives. This must have been the LBSCR's slowest and most obscure branch line. Here, a class D1 class 0-4-2T is threading a single wagon gingerly between road vehicles. The saloon cars and Mechanical Horse suggest a date in the 1930s. Have you tried Carmichael's coals? *Author's postcard collection*

Part 2 featuring the Cold Blow Tangle of branch lines to the north of New Cross Gate will appear in Issue 3 of Southern Times.

The LSWR G6 class

Back in steam days, some classes were immediately recognisable due to their design or by the sheer numbers built. On the Southern at least the Bulleid Pacific and Maunsell mogul types were probably some of the most regularly seen. Other classes might well be restricted to a particular area or limited in numbers with, examples being the R1 0-6-0T design which rarely if ever strayed from the South Eastern side, whilst at the opposite end of the system we may quote the E1/R 0-6-2T class which spent their days working from Exeter westwards.

In the middle of both we find the G6 class whose sphere of activity extended from London to Bournemouth and for a time as far west as Meldon although with the majority of engines that were numbered in capital stock concentrated in the central area.

The G6 design of 0-6-0T had its origins back in 1881 when a need was identified for a powerful shunting engine having six coupled wheels. William Adams, the Locomotive Superintendent of the London & South Western Railway, was '...unable to supply them...' (quote from Bradley but which we may take to mean there was either insufficient works capacity for construction at Nine Elms, or more likely insufficient resources for design. Had it simply been a case of works capacity then the new design could have been sent to a manufacturer to build).

Consequently Messrs. Beyer, Peacock were tasked with the construction of a further 12 engines of an existing type, the '330' class.

Further engines were needed 12 years later although by this stage a new design was

Formal portrait of No 258 dating from August 1894. This engine would survive until July 1961, a life just short of 67 years. The additional coupling chains may be noted whilst it also appears to have the vacuum brake this contradicting Bradley. ***Ian Wilkins collection***

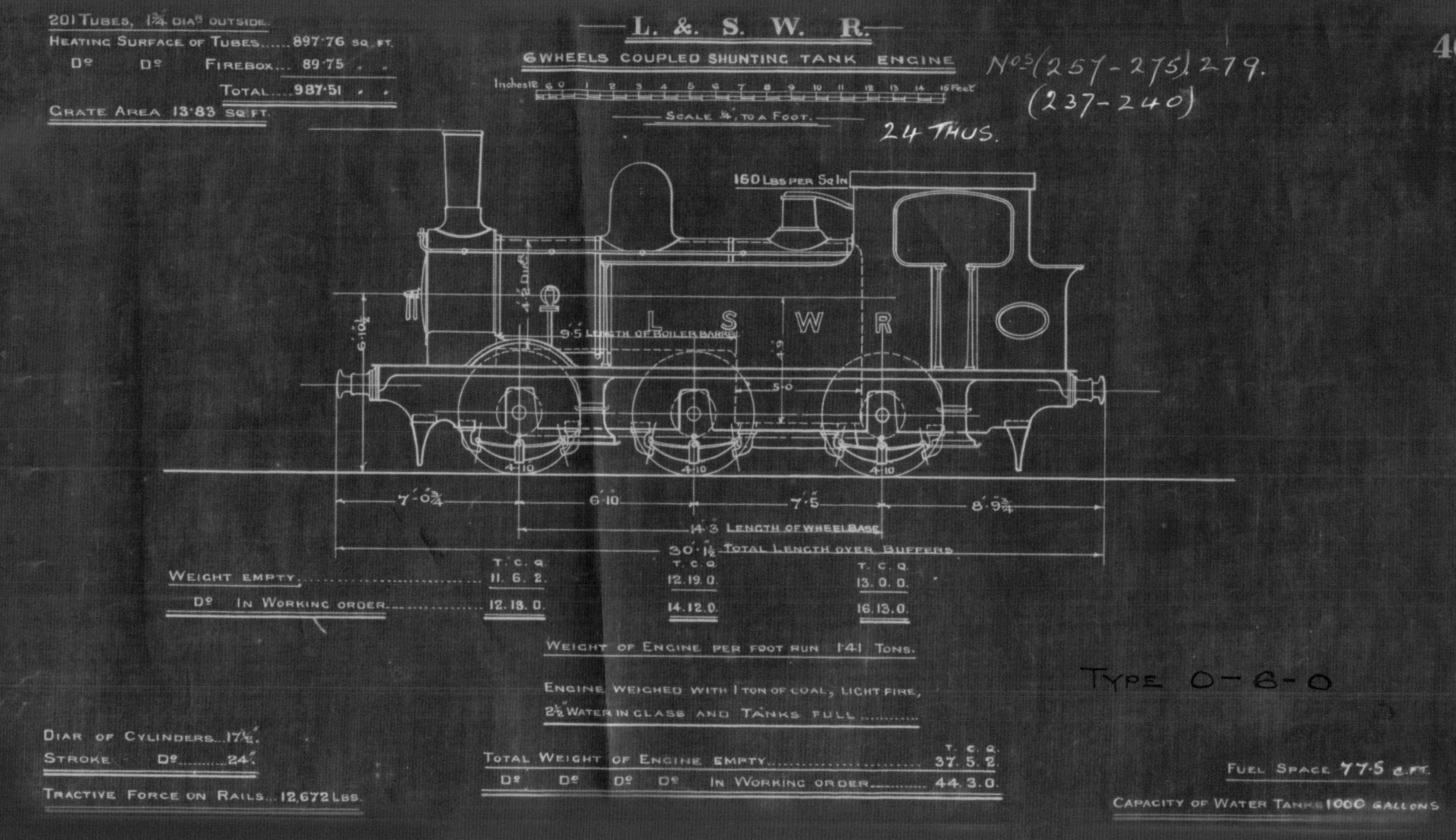

201 Tubes, 1¾ diaR outside.
Heating Surface of Tubes...... 897·76 sq. ft.
Dº Dº Firebox... 89·75 " "
Total.... 987·51 " "
Grate Area 13·83 sq. ft.
L. & S. W. R.
6 Wheels Coupled Shunting Tank Engine
Nos (257-275) 279.
(237-240)
24 THUS.
46
Inches 12 6 0 1 2 3 4 5 6 7 8 9 10 11 12 13 14 15 Feet
Scale ¼" to a Foot.
160 Lbs per Sq In
L S W R
4·2 Diar
9·5 Length of Boiler Barrel
6·10½
4·9
5·0
4·10
4·10
4·10
7·0¾
6·10
7·5
8·9¾
14·3 Length of Wheelbase
30·1½ Total Length over Buffers
T. C. Q.
Weight empty.......... 11. 6. 2. 12.19.0. 13.0.0.
Dº In Working order.......... 12.18.0. 14.12.0. 16.13.0.
Weight of Engine per foot run 1·41 Tons.
Engine weighed with 1 ton of coal, light fire, 2½" Water in glass and Tanks full..........
Type 0-6-0
Diar of Cylinders... 17½"
Stroke Dº.......... 24"
Tractive Force on Rails... 12,672 Lbs.
T. C. Q.
Total Weight of Engine Empty.......... 37. 5. 2.
Dº Dº Dº Dº In Working order.......... 44. 3. 0.
Fuel Space 77·5 c. ft.
Capacity of Water Tanks 1000 gallons

Just identified as LSWR No 277 at Strawberry Hill. The either direction sanding may be noted.

No 354 in SR days. This engine displays the addition of footboards and handrails which were fitted to engines working in, or had worked, at the Nine Elms yards. In SR days the prefix 'E' (indicating a Western Section engine) had also been carried for a time. It was also destined to be one having a short life; from June 1900 to November 1949. *The Transport Treasury*

available and ten engines, Nos 257 to 266 to be known as the G6 class, emerged from Nine Elms between June and October 1894. In many respects they were similar to the O2 0-4-4T class of a few years previous.

Despite in later years perhaps being considered small, they were compatible with contemporary similar machines from other railways with two inside cylinders, 160psi boiler pressure and a tractive effort of 17,235lbs.

In service the class quickly became popular in their intended shunting role, although, and again referring to Bradley, the exception was at Nine Elms where crews remained loyal to the older Beyer, Peacock design.

Just two years later and with more engines needed for the expanding trade at Southampton Docks, four more of the type were built, this time by Adams' successor, Drummond, in 1896. These additional machines served two purposes, firstly to replace a similar number of B4s sent to Southampton but also to provide larger engines in place of the B4 type on what been station pilot and yard shunter duties.

Interestingly with one exception, the boilers fitted to these engines, Nos 267 to 270, had been purchased from Beyer, Peacock a few years earlier in 1892 and had been intended to reboiler Beattie Well Tanks but had never been used. The exception was the last in the series, No 270, which received a boiler that had already seen service on an earlier Well Tank.

A further ten G6s were built in 1897 again using boilers from redundant Well Tanks. There were also differences with this latest build; longer smokeboxes, steam reversing gear, various (unspecified) footplate alterations, whilst aesthetically they were devoid of brass beading and had Drummond pattern numberplates.

Having successfully utilised what would otherwise have been considered potentially redundant boilers this time from more than one class, Drummond repeated the exercise with a final ten engines in 1900. The numbers given also now filled in some of the gaps in the allocated number series. This final batch were 160, 162, 276-8, 348, 349, 351, 353 and 354. The eventual number sequence for the complete class of 34 engines being 160, 162, 237 to 240, 257 to 279, 348, 349, 351, 353 and 354. One additional visual change with the final ten engines was the inclusion of a lipped chimney a-la Drummond style.

Engines built using salvaged boilers were originally designated the 'M9' class but the class type was standardised to 'G6' at the end of 1912.

Up to the time of grouping the following depots had an allocation:

Nine Elms – 7

Strawberry Hill – 5

Guildford – 3

Basingstoke – 1 (this worked the Park Prewett Hospital branch and also shunted to the Thornycroft Works).

Eastleigh – 8

Bournemouth – 1

Dorchester – 1

Salisbury – 2

Exmouth Junction – 5

One member of the class is not accounted for and may well have been an allowance for an engine considered under repair.

Their general task was shunting and local goods although those at Exmouth Junction also banked trains between the Exeter GWR and SR stations.

Not surprisingly banking duties involved maximum output and in consequence the coal capacity of the G6 design was found wanting and consideration was given to extending the bunkers – no doubt in similar fashion to what was later done with the O2 class – but this was deferred. What changes that did take place

Above: 278 about to start banking duty from Exeter St Davids to Exeter Queen Street. It was on this type of continuous work that coal supplies might run short. Special instructions applied as to the weights of passenger and goods trains that would require banking at Exeter starting with 36 wheels (axles) for passenger trains, seven hoppers and a van for ballast, or between 12-25 loaded wagons. ***Stephenson Locomotive Society***

Opposite top: G6 No 238 at Guildford and retaining its shunters' steps and handrails. Photographs indicate two types of coupling rods were carried, fluted rods on earlier engines and plain rods on later builds. No 238 was of the earlier build. Photographed on 3 March 1951, this was renumbered DS682 in November 1960 and would also be the final member of the class in service. ***The Transport Treasury***

Opposite bottom: No 237, the engine sold out of service and subsequently named (identified might be a more accurate description as we do not know if this was a painted designation or it was carried on a cast plate) ***Redbourn 30.*** **Seen here in SR days possibly at Eastleigh.** ***Stephenson Locomotive Society***

over the years were in effect minimal; chimney types, vacuum brake* (which necessitated adding weight to the front buffer beam so increasing the overall weight by around 4 tons) whilst boilers continued to be a mix of Drummond and Adams origin.

*Images from earlier appear to show a vacuum brake fitting although it was possible that not all were so fitted. This may be confirmed as No 263 is referred to as first fitted with the vacuum brake in May 1922 for trials on the Portland branch. These were not satisfactory and the equipment was removed – only to be reinstated on the whole class in a lengthy process between 1925 and 1947.

Post-grouping until 1941, allocations were much as they had been in earlier years although now no engines were shown at Strawberry Hill and instead three had appeared at Yeovil. The banking duty at Exeter had also been taken over by E1/R tanks although the G6 class still found a role in the yards at Southampton, Bournemouth and now Yeovil whilst the Eastleigh yards were almost the exclusive province of the G6 design.

The year 1941 saw No 269 sent to Reading as a possible addition / replacement to the existing Stirling built 0-6-0T class. There is slight confusion here as to whether this was for work in the SR or GWR yards. Whatever, the

SOUTHERN
237

No 30270, lipped chimney and no shunters' boards. Mention has already been made as to how one batch was referred to as being 'M9' classification; others were 'D9' – Nos 237 to 240, 'C7' – Nos 267 to 270, 'X7' – 271 to 275, 'D9' for No 279, and finally 'R9' for Nos 348 to 354. All were subsequently grouped under the 'G6' type. (Again refer to Bradley.) ***The Transport Treasury***

engine was apparently well liked and a second member of the class similarly transferred later in WW2. Certainly the class were regularly seen at Reading Southern later. It is believed Nos 258 and 260 were working in the area from February 1942. No 257 received minor (unspecified) damage in WW2 but no other details are known.

All 34 entered BR ownership – on paper at least – but many were in poor condition and consequently withdrawals commenced in August 1948 with five of the class laid aside. A further 14 went in 1949, two in 1950, and one in 1951, after which numbers remained stable until 1958 in consequence of a realisation there might otherwise soon be a shortage of shunting engines.

One was sold out of service, No 237 in 1949, which went to Richard Thomas & Baldwins Ltd of Redbourn Iron & Steel Works, Scunthorpe where it received the new identification *Redbourn 30*; the only member of the type also to ever carry a name. It was also modified with the removal of the vacuum brake and the fitting of a Wakefield mechanical lubricator. It worked until c1959 and was partly broken up two years later although the frames were salvaged for further internal use carrying scrap. Presumably the engine must have received some repairs after purchase or were some engines simply being withdrawn at the time still with an amount of useful life left?

One other, No 272, became DS3152 for service duties at Meldon Quarry in June 1950. It was replaced by No 30238 – renumbered DS682 in August 1960 until it too was withdrawn in December 1962.

Only one from the batch of early days BR withdrawals, No 30376, went for scrap carrying its BR number, the later survivors all receiving BR numbers. Livery under BR was plain black, just as it had been in post-1930 SR days, previous to which lining had been carried.

No 30277 at Reading SR and at this stage, 16 February 1958, also clearly in store – it survived until November 1961. BR classification was '2F'. It will also be noted the coupling was of the simple 3-link type. ***The Transport Treasury***

BR days also broke new ground with two members of the class now officially based at Templecombe although one of the Yeovil allocation had previously been out stationed here.

Withdrawals recommenced in 1958, diesel shunting engines able to undertake yard work more efficiently whilst in addition the G6 engines were by now generally well worn. With the exception of the former No 238 (DS682 at Meldon), the final three, Nos 30258, 30277, and 30349, went in 1961, DS682 following at the end of 1962. With their passing another Adams design disappeared as none were saved, although perhaps surprisingly considering their limited geographical use, mileages for two at least were over one million and which probably reflected similar totals for the remaining engines. In the case of No 348, this figure was achieved despite its 1948 withdrawal.

With grateful thanks to Gerry Nichols.

Bibliography – 'Locomotives of the LSWR Part 2'. By D. L. Bradley. RCTS. 1967.

Top: G6 No 30162 busying itself in the yards at Eastleigh on 8 November 1955. A member of the class based at Eastleigh would often find employment as the shed or works pilot. Mention has been made in the text of the single member of the class that was used at Basingstoke. At one point this was joined by a transferee from Exmouth Junction with the intention that 'passenger' trains (these were hospital workings as there was never a public service to Park Prewett Hospital) might be worked with a G6 at either end. However, a trial with two engines and five coaches proved too much on the steep 1-53 gradient allied to the sharp curve associated with the branch. *Eric Sawford / The Transport Treasury*

Bottom: No 30274 at Templecombe on 12 May 1958 looking as if it was not working at the time. *Stephenson Locomotive Society*

Opposite top: DS3152 (the former No 272) at Meldon Quarry on 26 March 1952; one of two of the class to be transferred to Departmental Duties (shunting) at Meldon. A small locomotive shed was provided here whilst repairs might be carried out at Exmouth Junction and overhauls at Eastleigh. Although not stated, it is likely another member of the class deputised at Meldon when necessary. Stephenson Locomotive Society

Opposite bottom: No 30274 again, this time at Bournemouth. This was one of a batch of five engines originally designated 'X7' and which had utilised boilers from withdrawn Beattie Well Tanks. *The Transport Treasury*

ENGINEERS DEPT
MELDON QUARRY
30058

Probably the end of the line for the former No 238, now DS682, at Eastleigh. The underframe is liberally covered in dust from its work at Melton whilst alongside is the former Lancing Works shunter DS680. Dominating the background is the new diesel depot, provided to service the fleet of DEMU sets and later the Class 33 and 73 locomotives. *Ken Wightman / The Transport Treasury*

No 30266 ex-works – the fluted rods will be noted – carrying a Salisbury '72B' shed code. Possibly one Salisbury duty for the type would be on the Market House branch and another shunting the yard at Fisherton. *The Transport Treasury*

Next time: the LSWR A12 0-4-2 class

"THE DRIVER BLEW UP AND THE SIGNAL CAME OFF—"

Extract from a letter received by the S.D.S.O. as interpreted pictorially in the *Southern Railway Magazine.*

Stephen Townroe's Colour Archive

On the basis the British climate is fickle to say the least and that this is being written whilst there is frost outside the window (Editor's excuse), we present some dramatic images of steam from the lens of Stephen Townroe with the intention of deliberately creating a shiver – well you might even be reading this when it is 90° in the shade. So, snow in summer...?

Taking good photographs in these conditions was not easy in film days and we have no doubt SCT had his share of failures as well.

Above: We start at Southampton Central on 27 January 1954 where U class 2-6-0 No 31624 is leaving with a train for Cheltenham via the MSWJ; considering the depth of snow on the coast did it even make it through the high Cotswolds? The coaching stock is all former GW, a 'Toplight' as the lead followed by two Collett vehicles. As with the 'Bournemouth Belle' departure, see page 50, only the starting signal is off, an indication perhaps that delays were occurring to a number of services.

Opposite top: This time it is a westbound Brighton – Bournemouth service on the same day with the motive power of the early 1950s for this working, an H2 Brighton Atlantic. No 32421 *South Foreland* in charge and seemingly leaking a bit of steam. Had the Leader design been successful, this was one of the regular turns the Southern Region Traffic Department had envisaged for the type; a study made of the water columns en-route to confirm they were of suitable height for 'the beast'.

Opposite bottom: From the opposite direction No 34069 *Hawkinge* arrives from Bournemouth, probably with a Waterloo service. Snow seems to have attached itself to two of the tender axleboxes – at least we know they are not running hot. One hopes the steam heat was working properly for the train as well. In all these images it is unlikely the timetable was being adhered to, but at least a service was being provided.

Opposite top: By rights it should be around 2.00pm but the leaden sky gives the impression it may well be somewhat later. No 35004 *Cunard White Star* is leaving Southampton Central with the down Bournemouth Belle but possibly only for a short distance as the distant signal for Millbrook remains stubbornly on.

Opposite bottom: We move now north and east to Brookwood in March 1955 where the cold atmosphere emphasises the steam escaping from the insides of T9 No 30724 as it departs with vans from Waterloo to Southampton. The occupied track circuit ahead of the starting signal has already restored the signal to 'on', the latter of the LSWR pneumatic type.

Above: Between Basingstoke and Southampton we have the impressive sight of what is probably an S15 (number not totally identified) working hard. On board the crew will be roasted on one side and freezing on the other, the concern in conditions such as this is that the water connections between tender and locomotive might freeze and so render the injectors inoperable. Consider also how far the photographer will have had to trudge to get his shot as well, and how long to wait?

Opposite top: This time we are at Woking still in early 1955 to witness No 30832 on an up van train and seemingly with steam to spare. From the look of the vehicles it is likely it was also running fully-fitted.

Opposite bottom: Still on the main line, another S15 seen across the water meadows at Allbrook heading north – destination either Nine Elms or Feltham. From the direction the exhaust is blowing there is an easterly wind present; no doubt a few choice words said when the crew were preparing the engine when faced with what we have called more recently ‘a beast from the east’.

Above: We continue now with a trip down the Alton line in similar conditions but moving forward to April 1958. Firstly the view at Butts Junction just south of Alton, once the divergence point of three routes; left to Fareham (the Meon Valley but by this time truncated at Farringdon), right towards Basingstoke (the remains of the light railway where ‘Oh Mr Porter’ was filmed), and looking straight ahead to Medstead & Four Marks, Ropley, Alresford, Itchen Abbas and the junction with the main line north of Winchester. The building on the right had once been the controlling signal box at Butts Junction, but was closed the top removed and found a new use as a permanent way hut in the 1930s.

Snow scenes between Alton and Winchester Junction.

Opposite top: The climb to Medstead & Four Marks. Considering the date, early 1958, the views were probably taken either from the front of a DEMU set or perhaps the driver's compartment of a pull-push set, whichever; one with a clean outlook!

Opposite middle; Leaving Medstead & Four Marks towards Ropley. From the footprints in the 'four-foot' the ganger appears to have already walked the line as would be his daily task.

Opposite bottom: The approach to Ropley and its famed topiary, but unlikely to be admired by many today. Even so the footprints indicate someone has been out and about, and from the look of the broomstick on the left, an effort has been made to keep the snow away from the siding points. A similar effort has been made on the platform in the area of the canopy where two intrepid souls await the warmth of the carriage.

This page, top: Leaving Ropley and once beyond the cutting on to an exposed section of line. Steam was sometimes preferable in conditions such as these, being able to force its way through lying snow without the risk of damaging delicate traction motors.

This page middle and bottom: Further south we have views of the cuttings beyond Alresford and with it some indication of the volume of snow accumulated. Likely a snow plough had passed this way but a blizzard or further wind could easily whip the lying snow on to the tracks again in moments. The bridge width is an indication the structure had been built for double track even if the earthworks were not.

Top: Return to civilisation at Winchester Junction. The train is curving around to join the main line and head south to Winchester, Eastleigh and Southampton. The railway cottages on the right were a feature for some years, the local signalman probably lived in one, but just like the branch and Winchester Junction signal box nothing now remains.

Bottom: South on the main line (well just about). The 2-car DEMU is waiting to take the branch but needs us to clear the single line first. The permanent way man may well have turned out to keep the points from freezing; regulations stating that in these conditions signalmen should operate points and crossings on a regular basis to reduce the likelihood of freezing when they were actually required. The diesel is a 2-car set, often the maximum permitted over the branch due to the gradients. On the immediate left, the bridge has the (GWR) Newbury – Winchester line passing directly underneath.

From the archives: Southern Signal Boxes Part 1 Some Power Box interiors

We are delighted to commence a series on Southern signal boxes starting with some sample interiors of power boxes.

Rationalisation and centralising signalling is not just a product of recent times as the Southern Railway had adopted this type of programme basically concurrent with its own electrification schemes. Even before this the LSWR had rationalised signalling on the main line between Brookwood and Basingstoke with power (pneumatically operated) intermediate block signals designed to increase line capacity.

So far as power operation was concerned, the benefits of concentrating resources on one location meant a saving of maintenance and of course staff at what would otherwise be several signal boxes. Disadvantages were the opposite, a fault or failure at the main structure could create havoc over a wide area.

The interiors illustrated appear to be principally 'one lever – one movement' rather than true 'route setting' where one lever might otherwise set up a complete route. (If we have got this wrong in the captions do please let us know!) True route setting 'entry-exit' type, would come with the next generation of signalling.

Clapham Junction 'B', brand new on 24 September 1952 and just less than three weeks before it was commissioned on 12 October. This was a 103 lever all electric installation controlling trains from Victoria on their way towards Brighton. A rearward facing frame is provided with the signalmen seemingly able to undertake most of their work sitting – although in practice this was not always the most comfortable operating position as a degree of stretching was required. It remained in use until 1980 when the area was incorporated into the Victoria signalling centre. ***British Railways***

The interior of the final signal box named Waterloo, brought into use on 18 October 1936. This behemoth took over the work of four mechanical boxes on the same day: Waterloo 'A', Waterloo 'B', Waterloo 'C', and Waterloo 'D'. Between the four mechanical boxes had been 408 levers, the new power frame structure incorporating a Westinghouse frame had 309 levers. The technical journal 'Modern Transport' referred to the new installation as 'Science in traffic operations…' and it certainly must have seemed that at the time. (There is a short sequence showing the signal box in operation in the excellent BTF film 'Terminus'.) After a life just short of 55 years, Waterloo was decommissioned on 30 September 1990, its physical position needed for the new Eurostar lines and platforms. *Southern Railway*

Another new box that took the work of others was at Woking. Photographed here on 25 June 1937, just two days before it went 'live', replacing Woking East, Woking Yard, and Woking Junction. The new box was sited at the west end of the island platform and remains standing today although out of use but listed. The two illuminated diagrams are different; one covering the east end and one the west end. Wooden case train describers are also installed. As yet certain other 'essential' equipment is wanting; chairs / stools for example. A panoramic view is provided on all sides but which also rendered such structures vulnerable in wartime. *Southern Railway*

Above: On the Brighton main line, we move south to Gloucester Road Junction and the 131 Westinghouse 'L' frame installed in the new box brought into use on 21 March 1954 and part of Stage 3 of the Central Section Colour Light Signalling Scheme. Photographed on 17 March 1954, four days before going 'live', again all is in place, the 131 lever frame fresh and new. It had an operational life of 30 years. *British Railways*

Opposite top: With two days of quiet left before all would be hustle and bustle as it came into use, this is South Croydon on 6 May 1955. 31 levers replacing at least one mechanical box having a greater number of mechanical levers thus confirming some dual operation was involved. Invariably this was the dual function of point movement and locking which would be confirmed by the lights behind. Only when these had been confirmed was the interlocking within the frame released and the lever able to be pulled to its full (reverse) position and the appropriate signal cleared. *British Railways.*

Opposite bottom: New Cross Gate, interior of the new signal box, on 29 September 1950. Train describer transmitters at either end and receivers on the wall alongside the diagram. Telephones at either end. This box was in use for 25 years. *British Railways*

SOUTH CROYDON

NEW CROSS GATE

Above: Victoria (Eastern) interior where slides are provided in place of levers although the function is identical. The alternate 'up' and 'down' positions was simply so that the length involved could be compressed. Note electric lighting is provided but with back up oil lamps suspended from the ceiling. This box contained 174 slides and had been brought into use as 'Victoria Yard' on 4 January 1920. It was renamed 'Victoria East' on 25 June 1939. ***Southern Railway***

Opposite page: Finally the interior of Forest Hill power box on 29 September 1950. 47 levers, Westinghouse 'L' frame and a service life of just under 19 years. Unusually the diagram hangs at an angle and is white on black – might this have been an experiment to assess which might be best in future? ***British Railways***

Next time: Power Box interiors

Sitting on the desk besides the keyboard as the captions to this article were being written, is this February 2022 release by Lightmoor Press.

Space precludes more than a brief mention of *'The Brighton line. Brighton to Coulsdon North. A Signalling Perspective',* by Chris Durrant.

What we can say in all honesty is it is casebound and copiously illustrated with black and white images on art paper; a 360 page monster and well worth every penny of the £45.00 cover price.

The publisher advertises it as a 'Limited Edition' and whilst signalling history is sometimes regarded as a specialist interest, I can promise this is far more than a technical treatise. I have no doubt it will become the standard work on the subject and consequently highly sought after.

Accident between Bearstead and Hollingbourne 20 August 1927 (The precursor to 'Sevenoaks four days later'.)

As is well known, on 24 August 1927 a tragic accident occurred near Sevenoaks when a Maunsell 'River' class 2-6-4T derailed at speed causing the deaths of 13 passengers. The engine was the 2-cylinder variant the class No 800 *River Cray*.

What may not be so widely known is that just four days previous, approximately 20 miles distant and again with the same class of engine, a similar derailment had occurred involving No 890 *River Frome*.

Unfortunately, in the case of this event it took time for Lt Col Mount to compile his report into what had occurred that day at Bearstead and Hollingbourne. However, looking back almost a century, had the information that subsequently came to light been known, Sevenoaks, four days later, might well have been prevented.

For Bearstead and Hollingbourne, The Board of Trade Investigating Officer was Lt Col Mount whilst the second event was dealt with by his colleague Maj Pringle.

Investigating officer's reports are invariably detailed and this one for Bearstead and Hollingbourne is no exception running to 22 sides. Not unnaturally it took some time for Lt Col Mount to compile his findings whilst the necessity for the considerable detail therein may well have been influenced by the second accident four days later.

Even so we do not consider a verbatim facsimile to be appropriate on this occasion and consequently we have taken extracts to cover the points raised. We should therefore first consider the service and make up.

The train concerned was the 10.51am passenger service from Charing Cross to Margate running via Maidstone East. The accident occurring about 12.23pm between Bearstead and Hollingbourne when travelling about 40mph. According to Lt Col Mount he was of the opinion the speed was '...probably more...'. (Other direct quotes from the official report will similarly be shown within inverted commas.) The derailment occurred approximately five furlongs beyond Bearstead and some 15 yards before reaching overbridge No 634.

In charge was No 890, the solitary 3-cylinder member of the River class, and with 11 vehicles behind the drawbar.

No 21	4-wheel covered carriage truck	8 tons
No 1296	Bogie third brake	30 tons
No 1303	Bogie composite	33 tons
No 1310	Bogie third brake	30 tons
No 918	Bogie third	21 tons
No 135	Bogie third	20 tons
No 597	6-wheel guard's van	13 tons
No 2018	Bogie third	20 tons
No 5369	Bogie composite	29 tons
No 5964	Bogie composite	21 tons
No 1820	4-wheeled luggage van	8 tons

Total 233 tons. Overall length about 376 feet.

'The Bissel truck of the engine remained on the road, the first wheels to become derailed (towards the 6-foot side) being those of the leading coupled axle. The remaining engine wheels immediately followed suit, as the result of subsequent rail displacement, the train was thus pulled foul of the up line, the right-hand rail being pushed outwards and the track ploughed up, a number of wheels becoming buried almost up to the axles. The train was brought to a stand in 166 yards, a little less than its own length, so that the van in rear and the rear bogie of the last coach but one remained on the road, the wheels not having reached the point where derailment commenced. The engine and first vehicle became separated from the rest of the train by a distance of roughly 9 feet.

K1 class 2-6-4T No 890 *River Frome,* the only three cylinder 'River' class tank engine and the engine involved in both the Bearstead and Maidstone derailments. The latter was a slow speed derailment as the engine was moving from the dock siding on the down side at Maidstone East to the locomotive shed on the up side. The conclusion of the report into this derailment was that engines of this class should be prohibited from using the dock siding. The derived drive for the centre cylinder will also be noted. Despite their obvious failings, the class were handsome machines. Sadly the subsequent Sevenoaks accident involving No 800 would have long lasting repercussions so far as the use of large tank engines on the Southern Railway / Region were concerned. Right up to the end of steam, enthusiasts' requests for the use of a 'W' class 2-6-4T were continuously declined.

'Apart from that suffered by the locomotive and rolling stock, some 400 chairs, 187 sleepers, and a couple of rails were broken or damaged.

'There were 150 to 200 passengers in the train, five of whom complained of minor injuries or shock. The guard was also shaken. The train came to a stand leaning towards the up road, the front portion being on high bank, and it was fortunate that derailment had not commenced towards the cess side. On the other hand the consequences might have been serious had the overbridge been supported by a central pier, the existence of which was mainly responsible for the regrettable casualty list in the case of the derailment at Sevenoaks four days later.

'The weather in August was very wet. It had rained on 14 out of 15 days prior to the accident, during which time (up to 9.00am on 20 August) 2.38 inches were recorded as having fallen at Maidstone. On the day in question 0.61 inches fell at Maidstone and 0.90 inches at Ashford, the majority probably subsequent to the derailment.'

For all practical purposes it may be said that the derailment occurred on the straight. We know that Mr Maunsell (CME) visited the scene.

So far as the permanent way was concerned this had been laid in 1883 and consisted of original 83lbs/yd double-headed Krupps rail which had decreased in weight through wear to 77.38lbs per yard. The rails had not been turned. Of note was that in 1923 an additional sleeper per rail was added and others were replaced by new or good second-hand ones, a total of 401 being put into the length of 1,980 yards, in the middle of which the derailment occurred. In 1924 a hundred more sleepers were used in this length, in 1925 fifty-one, in 1926 one, and this year up to the date of the derailment, nil.

'The cutting where the derailment occurred was known by repute, among others, to be a bad one, causing trouble in respect of track maintenance in wet weather with clay spewing up at the ends of the sleepers. This was removed three years ago over the whole width of the cutting to a depth of 3 inches, below sleepers, ashes being employed to take its place; but during last winter the clay worked up again, and it was showing in certain places in the cess of the down line and also between sleepers, as the result of the heavy rainfall preceding the accident.'

Of particular interest in the report were statements from the men on the ground appertaining to their local experience. 'Ganger J. Shorter, a man of 30 years' service, for the last five of which he had been in charge of the Bearsted gang, was away on a week's leave at the time of the accident; but he was due to take up patrol duty again on the following day, Sunday. Sub-ganger F. Bills was therefore in charge at the time with the remaining three men, the length comprising two miles of double line and three sidings at the station.

'In heavy rain, which more or less continued throughout the day, Bills commenced to walk the length at 7am and returned via the down road, passing (what was) the site of the derailment at about 8.45am, before reaching the station for breakfast. At about 10.30am he again walked towards Hollingbourne, past the site, accompanied by the gang, to deal with a portion of track where the bank tended to slip (a constant source of trouble at this particular place in wet weather) a short distance ahead of the cutting in question. The gang left there at about 11.45am passing the site once more, and returned to the station at noon.

'Bills had noticed "nothing wrong" with the track in the cutting, though it is a place to which particular attention is paid ......and he was confident that had there been any serious out of level on the curve he would have seen it. He stated that in wet weather the curve required attention as often as two or three times a week, and on the Monday of the week concerned a few slack places had been dealt with. Again on Thursday the 18 "when dealing with this curve we lifted in places to an inch and a half. We lifted on ashes with the material that was in the road and with a certain amount of ashes that we had on the up road. We did not trolley any ash in on Thursday, probably we did this a month ago. I was lifting to eye and did not use a level board or spirit level;...was simply lifting low spots to bring them up to the level of the road on either side, the length in each case perhaps extending to 13 or 14 sleepers.

"While we were lifting on Monday and Thursday the previous week we pulled in the track on the curve to the extent of half an inch. This particular curve tends to go out in wet weather." On the days in question he noted, by eye, the amount of super-elevation that existed when his lift was finished, and he judged it to be a full inch, and in this connection he added that nobody had instructed him "in regard to the amount of super-elevation on this curve, but we try to keep it an inch up." He said that Permanent Way Inspector Ashman inspected the curve on the previous Monday when the gang were working on it, and "he is fully aware of the defects of this point." Ganger Shorter subsequently confirmed Bills' evidence with regard to the frequency with which this curve required attention in wet weather, He was satisfied up to the time he went on leave that "the road was perfectly safe "; but on the other hand the conditions in respect particularly of the clay in the foundation had apparently been on his mind for a long time, and he stated that he had had discussions with Inspector Ashman on the subject, though when examined on the subject he was unable even roughly to indicate when such discussions occurred or what was said.

'In regard to his maintenance generally, and particularly to the number of loose spikes subsequently found in the road, he admitted that responsibility in this respect was his; but stated "I thought that the road was to have been renewed, and that is one reason for not replacing the spikes. Another reason is that owing to so much wet weather, we have had other work to do and have not had sufficient

K class 2-6-4T No 790 *River Avon* on mixed stock. The size, particularly the height, of the design is exemplified here against the early stock, the formation showing the insertion of several luggage vans in between the passenger vehicles.

time. We have plenty of spikes in the station and material was at hand, This respiking would have taken us a week. At different times my gang have had to be called away to unload ballast trains, but I have never complained that my gang is not up to strength." He referred also to work on the section generally being behind......suggesting that it was the result of short time following the industrial dispute of last year... .'

Mr Ashman expressed satisfaction in regard to the maintenance generally of Shorter's length, having dealt with the removal three years ago of the clay in the bed and the introduction of further ashes; but apparently he did not realise that the curve required attention two or three times a week in wet weather.

Chief (Permanent Way) Inspector Mr Tipton .... Was not consulted before the heavy engines commenced to run on this line. His opinion was that the road was "fit for the 'King Arthur' class or the 'Lord Nelson' at a speed of 50 miles an hour. It is a decent old road", but he objected strongly to the 'River' class, and his views in respect of these engines, particularly No 890, will be mentioned later.

Mr Shaw, the Divisional Engineer, was also questioned and commented that with hindsight had he known the condition of the track he would have imposed a speed restriction of 15 miles per hour for all traffic. Based, however, upon personal observations of the rolling movements of 'River' class engines, compared with other types, and upon the reports of his inspectors and gangers, he was strongly of the opinion that no engine, other than that of the 'River' class, would have become derailed on this occasion at 40 miles per hour, though he agreed that the four-wheeled tender engine, E Class No 587 hauling the preceding passenger train which passed over the site 15 minutes previously, "did not go over without risk." Next came a damning comment: "From my inspectors' reports the road (generally) is more knocked out of line by this ('River ') class of engine than any other.....the 'River' class engines knock the road crooked. They certainly find the weak spots in the road."

Mr Upton held stronger views still, "I do object to the 'River' class engines over this road owing to the tremendous rolling at high speeds. All observation is that they roll generally on good road or bad. I hold the opinion that No 890 is a very bad engine." He continued. "It is the opinion of the inspectors and gangers that these engines knock the road

Another 2-cylinder engine, this one No 804 *River Tamar* which ran in the form seen for less than two years from September 1926 to June 1928 after which it was rebuilt as a 2-6-0 tender locomotive.

about more than the other classes of engines. I cannot say definitely that this has actually been noticed: it is a mere guess on account of the rolling. On a good British standard road, well ballasted, the 'King Arthur' engines ride smoothly, while those of the 'River' class are all over the place. They appear to roll immensely. We always reckon the 'River Frome' worse than the other 'River' class. I have seen that roll tremendously and much worse than the other 'River' class."

We now bring into the conversation Mr Elson, the SR's Chief Engineer. "With a normal engine I really do not see why it should have derailed. Although I have no doubt the deformation of the road contributed to this derailment, I should not have expected a normal engine passing at a speed of 40 miles per hour to be derailed. Looking at its history I am afraid I cannot come to any other conclusion than that engine No 890 is abnormal. All the information I have is that it rolls heavily."

Lt Col Mount then makes reference to a previously unknown incident from 31 March 1926 again involving No 890 which derailed when hauling a passenger train at Wrotham. That investigation revealed the engine was rolling prior to the site of the derailment which again occurred in a cutting where drainage was poor and again it was very wet.

As a direct result of the 1927 derailment the 'River' class were withdrawn whilst the track in the area was relaid and the super-elevation increased.

At this stage the general feeling of the Engineering Department was that both the 1926 and 1927 accidents were primarily due to an inherent defect in the riding of this particular engine, No 890, and that the latter case served if anything to confirm this view.

Lt Col Mount then spent some time describing the engine type itself, its origins, build, features with particular emphasis on the springing, and the work the class had been put to.

We need not concern ourselves with these titles on this occasion and the reader is instead referred to the excellent RCTS volume 'Locomotives of the South Eastern & Chatham Railway' by D. L. Bradley from 1980.

Suffice to say that the majority of the class dated from 1925/26 and apart from working trains on the former SECR main line had also worked between London and Brighton, also cross country between Reading and Redhill. Riding qualities generally were noted as improved when running bunker first but drivers preferred to run looking forward and consequently the advantage of the tank engine in not requiring to be turned at the end of the journey was lost.

It has been common in recent years for the enthusiast fraternity especially to think of little else other than their tendency to roll at speed when referring to the class, but a comment from Lt Col Mount may abrogate these views. 'From the 12 December 1925, until 31 March 1927, the date of the Wrotham derailment, the mileage worked by No 890 amounted to 37,405;and subsequently, up to the time of the Bearsted derailment, 10,504. In respect of this service I understand that no reports of rolling, or in fact of any kind relating to steadiness and efficiency on the road, had been made or received, except for the evidence already mentioned following the Wrotham accident.

Following Bearstead No 890 was the subject of a meticulous examination and no defects or undue wear was found likely to have been a contributory feature.

We turn now to evidence from footplate crews, starting with that of the two previous trains running on the same section of line. Both the engines on these services were of the tender type.

'Driver G. Francis, of the former train, stated that he felt nothing abnormal as he approached the bridge and there was no lurching when passing round the curve. He had had no occasion to make reports in respect of the road at this point. Driver Hamden, of the latter train, similarly could remember nothing unusual in the running of his engine over the site. He also had never had any cause to complain about the section of line in question; and said he noticed no difference in running between the portions of new and old road respectively approaching and after leaving Bearsted. In fact, in his experience, 27 years on the Eastern section, he said there was no difference in this respect from the main line.

Hamden had only driven 'River' class engines on the main line, and had handled No 890, on the last occasion, some eight weeks previous to the accident. He had noticed no difference between its behaviour on the road and that of others (Nos 807-809). Generally, on good track, he considered that, as a class, they rode better than tender engines of the F.1, D and E classes. But he stated that "it seems to me that when they strike a bad place in the road then rolling commences, and if it is rather more than I like I generally apply the steam brake; this rolling takes place at about 60 miles an hour; but at 40 m.p.h. I have not noticed it." He had only once, when driving No 808, experienced a, "bump at the end of the roll," speed being then 60 m.p.h. (viz., at Grove Park when driving the 8.35am train from Ashford on the 4 August). Mr Rodgers, of the Chief Mechanical Engineer's Department, was riding upon the footplate at the time for the purpose of special observation, and I understand that this location and others, viz., mile posts 11, 21, where rolling was also noted on this particular journey, were brought to notice.'

We come now to the evidence of Driver C. Cummings, a man with 25 years' experience in his role and who was in charge of No 890 at Bearsted. Driver C. Cummings was in charge of the train in question. 'He stated he was running about nine minutes late but was not making up time. He estimated that, speed when passing through Bearsted was 30mph and that with steam applied (the little valve being open and the engine running normally) this increased on the falling gradient approaching the bridge to 40mph. He could give little information in regard to the circumstances of the derailment itself as he said that he received no warning.....there was no previous heavy swaying when passing round the curve approaching the bridge, and, in fact, the engine "was riding very steadily, the speed being low." He heard no unusual noise, but apparently a sudden rocking took place and he felt "the train riding badly," when he promptly applied the vacuum brake.

'He was of the same opinion as driver Hamden in respect of the tendency of the "River class to roll at high speed where the road lies low or is not so good as in other parts "; but he had not noticed it particularly in the locality of the cutting in question, speed there being usually low. He referred to certain points on the Eastern Section to confirm his experience that these engines, as a class, felt track defects more than others, and he said that he took the usual action to stop undue motion by closing the regulator and applying the steam brake. He had not observed much difference in this respect with tanks full or empty. He had not, however, reported any of the cases to which he referred, for the reason that "the road generally seems to be good," and "I have always taken it very carefully through places that I knew were bad."'

Lt Col Mount's report contained further evidence from other drivers, both of their handling of the class and also when driving at that particular location.

The report then turned to describe the trials of No 890 that took place following repairs and on the LNER and SR – *we intend to describe these in some detail in issue 3 of ST.*

Finally we have Lt Col Mount's conclusions. 'The main conclusion therefore to be drawn in respect of the foregoing evidence relating to the unsteadiness on the road of engine No 890 and, in fact, also of others of the "River" class which has been experienced and noticed respectively by drivers and the engineering staff, is that imperfections in the track must have been primarily responsible for the movements described and seen. And in my opinion it follows that the derailments at Wrotham and Bearsted were initiated accordingly.

'In regard to the former case there is conflict of opinion in respect of the reasons for the subsequent withdrawal of the engine and others of this class; but I can only conclude that the partial derailment on that occasion came about as the result of irregularity of super-elevation and instability of the ballast bed, following saturation by heavy rain, severe rolling and nosing of this heavy engine at high speed being thereby set up, with the result that the flange of the leading coupled wheel on the inside of the sharp curve in question was lifted and traversed the rail. The engine, however, at that time was not fitted with flat centres upon the bissel and bogie trucks, which had been shown to make for "very great improvement" in steadiness of riding, and thus its sympathy to the comparatively minor track defects, which on that occasion existed, was perhaps more pronounced than it might otherwise have been.

'The track in the cutting in question lacked the essential attribute of "permanent" way, viz., stable and efficiently drained foundation. It could only, therefore, have been reasonably relied upon to support, with safety, light and slow-speed traffic during a continuous period of wet weather such as had been experienced. The evidence of the ganger, relating to the frequency with which attention had to be paid to it, emphasises the general conditions which prevailed. But perhaps the state of affairs at the time can best be gauged by Mr Shaw's opinion that the site should not have been traversed by any traffic at more than 15 miles an hour.

'On the evidence also of the ganger and Permanent Way Inspector it is difficult to resist the conclusion that maintenance generally was behind hand, in view of pressure of other work in the neighbourhood, and the knowledge that it was proposed to relay the road next year. Nevertheless, having carefully considered the circumstances, I do not think that responsibility can reasonably be attached to anyone individually. The conditions in the cutting were well-known to those directly concerned, but it appears that the capability of this old road to carry the modern loading, which had been authorised, was entirely misjudged, in respect more particularly or the stability of its foundation in wet weather. In fact, it would seem that such authorisation, which included not only the "River" but the " King Arthur " class of engine and the " Lord Nelson ", is open to the general criticism that too much was being expected of the ordinary gang, particularly when, as was apparently the case, the men had other than purely track maintenance duties to perform, and a considerable length of road of this character to contend with.'

Lt Col Mount then spoke of the comparative weights that existed on the driving wheels of the derailed train compared with the previous services. 'There is little doubt that such concentration of loading on a comparatively short wheel base, at a speed of certainly not less than 40 miles an hour, simply increased the subsidence which was already in process of developing'.

The start of this article referred to the time that has passed since, namely almost 100 years, and in consequence we may look back objectively and consider further the conclusions that might be drawn. Firstly there can be no doubt the permanent way on parts of the South Eastern was poor and certainly not able to stand up to the rigours of the 'River' class. Whether George Ellson (1875-1949) was truly the man to act as scapegoat is still open to question, perhaps his remit as Chief Engineer of the whole Southern Railway was simply too great a task for just one man. Whatever, we know he retained an aversion for running large tank engines on passenger trains for the rest of his tenure, Sevenoaks in particular continuing to haunt him thereafter.

Richard Maunsell meanwhile appeared to weather the storm slightly better, despite, according to Clapper, being instructed (this was after the subsequent riding trails) by the General Manager Sir Herbert Walker to rebuild

No 793 *River Ouse* dwarfs its train in SR days. Holcroft was complimentary about the steaming capabilities of the class but having praised their abilities makes little reference to their weaknesses. *Stephenson Locomotive Society*

the 'River' class in more conventional tender engine form. Two at least being stored at Reading until called to works. In this guise as useful members of the 'U' class (and now unnamed) they performed sterling service almost to the very end of steam.

In both cases we might even raise the comment, was the 'Chief' simply unaware or at that time in history simply unapproachable when it came to communication from the lower levels.

At the same time as the rebuilding of the engines was concerned, a process of re-ballasting the whole of the former SE section boat train routes was put in place.

Holcroft adds little to the story, commenting on the facts and in general terms praising the steaming and haulage abilities of the class but makes no mention of their rolling. He does add that previously No 890 had also derailed in a siding with a sharp curvature at Maidstone, '...and not on the road at speed.' He adds, 'The only question was whether the engine had suffered damage in some way which was not detected, but nothing was found to suggest it.'

Wrotham, Bearstead and then Sevenoaks were lessons hard learnt, sadly 40 years later in 1967 they had be to relearnt again after Hither Green. The punishing effect not this time of steam, but diesel and electric units, on trackwork failing to be recognised until it was too late.

Only four days after Bearstead and Hollingbourne came this; the Sevenoaks accident, this resulting in several fatalities. Whether earlier realisation as to the possible cause might have been able to prevent the derailment is unlikely for at that time the various contributory factors had all not been understood. Sevenoaks remains the one that should not have happened. *Jeremy Cobb*

U class 2-6-0 No 31807, the former K class 2-6-4T No A807 River Axe, seen here in BR service and in what was sadly all too common 'grime' livery. Originally built at Brighton as a tank engine in November 1926, it was destined to have a short life in tank engine form before being taken back to Brighton for conversion in March 1928 having run 25,376 miles. It was released to traffic, now nameless in June 1928, renumbered 1807 in January 1931 and finally became No 31807 in July 1948. During it s BR life it saw service from Redhill, Stewarts Lane, Feltham, Norwood Junction and Three Bridges before returning to Stewarts Lane in July 1962 from where it was withdrawn in January 1964. Ken Wightman / Transport Treasury

The story of the 'River' class will continue in Issue 3 with details of riding trials both before and after 'Sevenoaks'

From the archives: Photo feature: Southern 2/3 car DEMUs

Like them or loath them, the 2/3 car DEMU sets that operated on the Southern Region for in excess of 40 years were a feature that many will remember.

Born out of a need to replace steam on lines not at the time considered worthwhile for electrification, their initial introduction was greeted with both acclaim and criticism. Acclaim as here was a modern (sic) replacement for what was seen as an old fashioned steam train, but criticism over the noise and vibration experienced when travelling in the power car and the restricted toilet facilities when the sets were used on longer distance wordings; which had never been the original intention.

We see here three sets in variations of green livery working in the Hampshire area.

Above: Entering St Denys from the direction of Portsmouth is unit 1130 with a Portsmouth to Andover service, via Southampton Central. Portsmouth - Andover services also operated via Botley and Eastleigh but which carried a '54' headcode. ***Graham Smith courtesy Richard Sissons***

Opposite top: All the original Hampshire sets were originally built with just two cars but this was soon changed with the exception of Nos 1120-1122. (No 1122 was rarely seen in Hampshire working instead within Sussex / Kent.) Here 2-car set No 1122 is at Alresford waiting to depart towards Alton. Only limited first class accommodation was provided - two compartments - identified by the yellow band at cantrell level. The yellow warning panel was a step towards full yellow ends, the yellow handrails rather rarer. Nos 1120 and 1121 were regular performers on this steeply graded line. ***Graham Smith courtesy Richard Sissons***

Opposite bottom: Temporarily running without its centre coach, unit 1124 is heading west towards Totton probably around 1966/67 and still in green livery - the third-rail is in place. The '03' headcode' does not appear in any list we have located whilst close examination appears to show some passengers on board. ***Roger Holmes 4571***

ALRESFORD

1120
31
20
WINCHELSEA

Opposite top: We move east now to Hailsham with No 1120 on the Polegate - Hailsham shuttle service sometime between 14 June 1965 and 9 September 1968. The former date was when passenger services on the Cuckoo line north of Hailsham had ceased and it was only ever going to be a matter of time before Hailsham too succumbed. Track here was lifted in 1969 the site remaining moribund for some years before being redeveloped for housing and as a car park. *Graham Smith courtesy Richard Sissons*

Opposite bottom: 'Sussex' unit No 1303 arriving at Winchelsea. These - all 3-car sets - were built at Eastleigh in 1962, and having a similar power unit also quickly acquired the nickname 'Thumpers' - due to the noise from the engine. The Sussex trains were designed for a dual role, intended for both medium distance working between London Victoria to Uckfield and Eridge as well as branch line duties in the county. Consequently in these sets there was more first class accommodation which was positioned in the centre coach. Other design differences included a more rounded roof end and insets for the multiple unit connections. The yellow patch has already been mentioned; the black triangle an indication to platform staff which end of the train had the luggage accommodation; which was positioned within the guard's compartment. *Graham Smith courtesy Richard Sissons*

Above: For its final years of public service, the only crossing place on the Mid Hants line between Winchester Junction and Alton was at Alresford and where we see 2-car No 1122 waiting for the signal to depart north and 3-car No 1133 soon to proceed south in early 1970. BR all over blue and full yellow ends now apply whilst it will be noted No 1133, which was a slightly later build, has a modified route indicator blind window. ('43' was the headcode for trains between Southampton and Alton.) Although originally working various branch services only, the Hampshire sets quickly migrated to cross-country lines including Reading to Basingstoke with some services from Reading extended to Salisbury or Portsmouth. It was also not unknown for a unit to work a stopping service beyond Salisbury - this being the time when the former SR main line had been reduced to secondary status. On such longer workings turns the lack of toilet facilities and gangways between vehicles was heavily criticised. To accommodate extra parcels accommodation, certain of the 'Hampshire' units later had the seats removed from the former single second class compartment located between the driver's cab and the first class accommodation. *Roger Holmes 6948*

It is our intention to cover the 'Tadpoles' units at a later date.

Treasures from the Bluebell Railway Museum Tony Hillman

An LBSCR Terrier

Reading the title most of you will assume that the Terriers are the Bluebell engines *Stepney* and *Fenchurch*. But there other Terriers and they are not the dogs either.

The Terrier to be mentioned here is a large leather-bound book containing plans of the railway lines when originally built or soon afterwards. This version of the word Terrier comes from the Latin Terra meaning earth and the dictionary definition states that a Terrier is a register of lands belonging to a landowner.

The Railway Companies produced these Terriers to include a detailed map of the line along with, in some cases, the previous owners. More details show where land had been purchased in areas larger than required for the line with the unwanted parts sold off. In many cases the ownership of adjoining land was specified.

The Terrier shown here was produced in June 1906 at a scale of 2 chains (44 yds) to an inch. William Forbes, named on the cover, was General Manager of the LBSCR from 1899 until he retired at the Grouping. The pages are cleverly laid out so that when opened out they follow the often-curvy nature of the line.

WILLIAM FORBES ESQ.

LEWES, UCKFIELD
& TUNBRIDGE WELLS LINE
SECTION 1
(LEWES TO BUXTED)

The plan shown is of Uckfield station. There is a large amount of detail. The half mile mark in the middle of the station is the 16½ mile post, the LBSCR marked its distances from Brighton. The line to Uckfield was opened in October 1858 by the Lewes and Uckfield Railway, being absorbed into the LBSCR six years later.

The land owner either side of the station is Richard James Streatfield (spelt Streatfeild) on the plan. He was a Justice of the Peace and owned much land and property in Uckfield. He was born in 1844 and so was a minor when the land was sold to the Railway, James Brown his guardian looking after his interest.

The area owned by the LBSCR is shown within the pink border. The blue bordered parts being previously owned but sold. Within four months of opening the piece of land marked as the Bridge Hotel was sold to Thomas Merricks (F,G,H,J & K on the plan). Land at the Gas Works was also sold to the gas company while the gas company sold land to the Railway (A, B & C). Some effort was also made to keep the plan updated as a pencil annotation was added when the crossover between the platforms was removed in 1946.

The Museum Archive contains Terriers from many areas of Southern England. The one used here, along with two others, were recently donated to the Archive from the Isle of Wight Railway Archive. We thank them for passing them to us.

Editors note: 'Treasures from the Bluebell Railway Museum' is intended to be a regular series in Southern Times, kindly compiled by Assistant Curator Tony Hillman.

The Bluebell Railway Museum, located on Platform 2 at Sheffield Park, is well worth a visit and is a veritable treasure trove of artefacts and ephemera from the Southern Railway and its constituents. We look forward to featuring more treasures in the next issue.

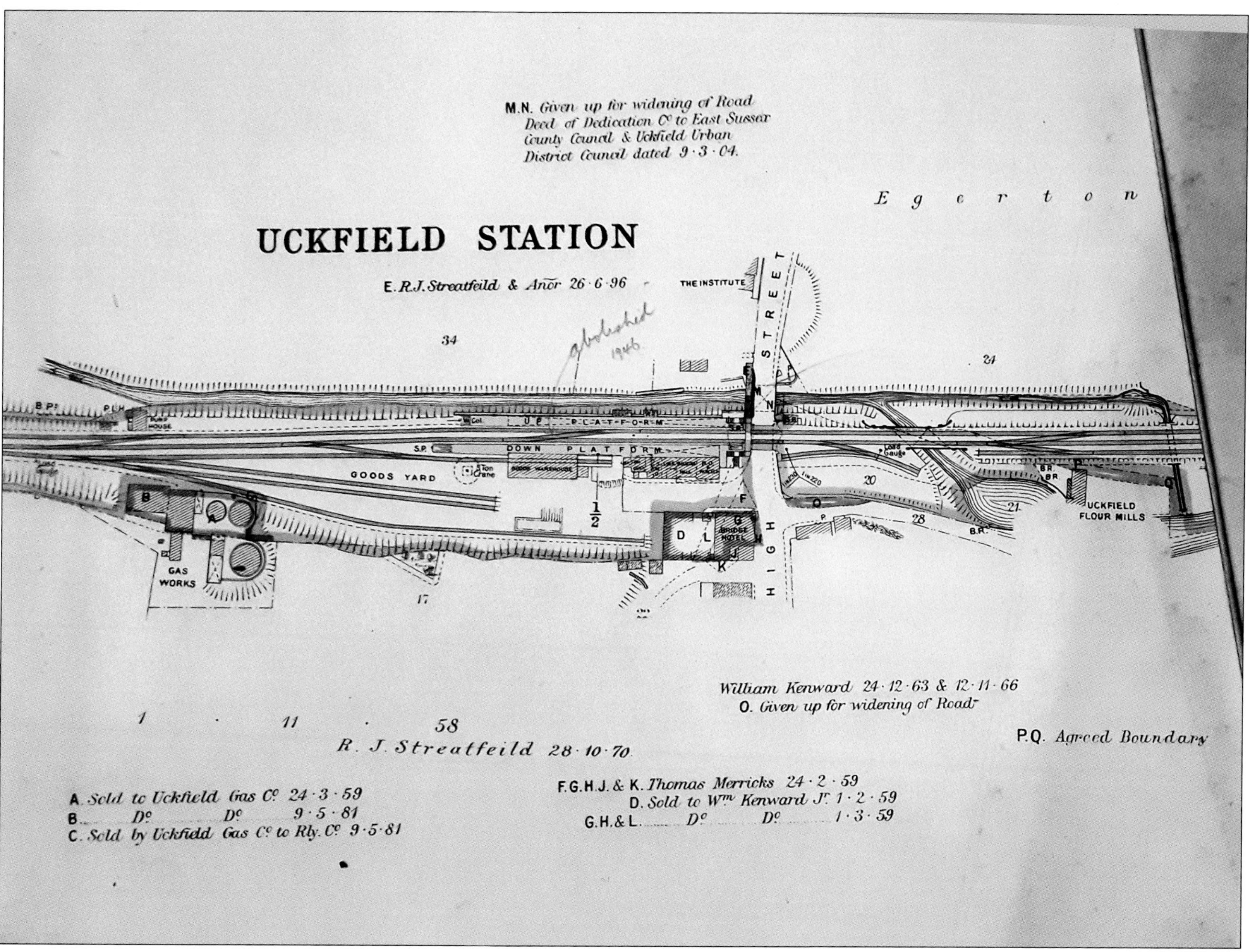
M.N. Given up for widening of Road
Deed of Dedication Co to East Sussex
County Council & Uckfield Urban
District Council dated 9·3·04.
E g e r t o n
UCKFIELD STATION
E. R.J. Streatfeild & Anor 26·6·96
THE INSTITUTE
STREET
HIGH
34
24
UP PLATFORM
DOWN PLATFORM
GOODS YARD
GOODS WAREHOUSE
PUMP HOUSE
GAS WORKS
BRIDGE HOTEL
UCKFIELD FLOUR MILLS
Load Gauge
20
21
28
17
1/2
William Kenward 24·12·63 & 12·11·66
O. Given up for widening of Road
1 · 11 · 58
R. J. Streatfeild 28·10·70
P.Q. Agreed Boundary
A. Sold to Uckfield Gas Co 24·3·59
B. Do Do 9·5·81
C. Sold by Uckfield Gas Co to Rly. Co 9·5·81
F.G.H.J. & K. Thomas Merricks 24·2·59
D. Sold to Wm Kenward Jr 1·2·59
G.H.& L. Do Do 1·3·59

From the footplate

Firstly, thanks to those who have kindly written in with kind comments and constructive suggestions. A few have pointed out the (not) deliberate mistake re the cover caption on Issue 1. Yes, we got the cover caption wrong and yes, we noticed it too late to stop it happening. The 'Merchant Navy' view was substituted for the 'Schools' at the last moment, and of course it was intended the caption would be changed ... So blame all of us involved, simply put, no one spotted it. What should have appeared as the caption is simply, 'Schools, No 905 *Tonbridge* at the rear of Eastleigh shed being prepared for a boiler washout.'

Several readers have also been touch on other topics, we start with Martin James 'Hello Southern Times. I enjoyed the first edition ... I hope the following will be of interest. ... The location of the photo on the top of page 26 is Boscombe Station. The overbridge carries Ashley Road ... and a tramway traction pole - which was in the middle of the road - can clearly be seen. The location of the photo on page 29 is Bodmin North. For some reason the H12/H13 is in the yard on the third line from the platform. The ramshackle building in the background is on the goods shed road - vans having to come through the goods shed for loading / unloading....'.

We have also been fortunate enough to receive 'best wishes for the future' notes from a number of readers, we will mention just a few by name; Bill Allen, Christopher Fifield, Colin Martin, Tony Teague, Alastair Wilson amongst others. Gentlemen, thank you all.

We were recently passed the original of the above from Barry Coombe. Official view of No 35004 *Cunard White Star* of course (with white buffers), and with the addition of the signature of the great man in the bottom corner. On the reverse is the 'Southern Railway Copyright Free' stamp, the date of 9 January 1942 and the reference A3363. Possibly this was one of several prints circulated and the original owner subsequently met Mr B and simply asked him to sign it.